Craig Dearden-Phillips

YOUR CHANCE TO CHANGE THE WORLD

The No-fibbing Guide to Social Entrepreneurship

In association with:

DIRECTORY OF SOCIAL CHANGE

school for
social
entrepreneurs

Published by
Directory of Social Change
24 Stephenson Way
London NW1 2DP
Tel. 08450 77 77 07; Fax 020 7391 4804
E-mail publications@dsc.org.uk
www.dsc.org.uk
from whom further copies and a full books catalogue are available.

Directory of Social Change is a Registered Charity no. 800517

First published 2008

ISBN 978 1 903991 93 0

British Library Cataloguing in Publication Data
A catalogue record for this book is available from the British Library

Illustrations by Grizelda
Cover and text designed by Kate Bass and Simon Parkin
Typeset by Linda Parker
Printed and bound by Page Bros., Norwich

All Directory of Social Change departments in London:
08450 77 77 07

Directory of Social Change Northern Office:
Courses and conferences 0845 77 77 07
Research 0151 708 0136

Contents

Dedication

I would like to dedicate this book to Katy, Ruby and Wilfred,
and also to all those who have backed me with their time
and money when all I could offer them was a vision.

Acknowledgements

I wish to thank all of the people who allowed me to ask them questions during the writing of this book. I have been really warmed by the generosity and encouragement shown by my fellow social entrepreneurs.

I would also like to thank Fred Heddell and Phil Tatt, the Chairpersons of Speaking Up, for giving me some time off in 2007 to write, John Martin at DSC for his patience, support and good humour during the writing and Charlotte Chambers of the School for Social Entrepreneurs for reviewing my early draft.

However, my greatest thanks go to Mark Griffiths of Ideal Word, whose encouragement and many hours of pro-bono editorial support has helped my voice and that of others to shine through. The shape and energy of this book owes much to Mark's talent and ideas.

Social entrepreneurs who helped to write this book

RICHARD ALDERSON Previously a management and technology consultant, Richard made a career change to the social entrepreneurship sector in 2003. He conceived the idea for Careershifters – which helps people to create a career that truly excites them – while making his change. www.careershifters.org

MARTIN CLARK Martin is the founder of a new social enterprise incubator in Cambridge. He has also set up a number of new social initiatives in inner cities throughout the UK. Martin works for Citylife, whose mission is to be at the forefront of developing social investment mechanisms that enable organisations, businesses and local people to finance solutions to disadvantage in their own communities. www.citylifeltd.org

DOUG CRESSWELL A former council manager, Doug founded Pure Innovations, a not-for-profit company that delivers supported employment and day care for a number of councils across Greater Manchester. In line with its goal of bringing a fresh approach to modernising traditional services, the company runs café bars, an art/conference centre and a radio station.

HANNAH EYRES Hannah runs Keyfund, which finances and supports young people to complete projects based on their own ideas. This is achieved through a network of training, member facilitators and access to project funding. www.keyfund.org.uk

SIMON FENTON-JONES Simon runs Streetshine, which provides shoe-shining services to businesses in the City of London. 'Shiners' are recruited from homeless backgrounds, given full training and then assisted to set up their own franchise as an independent shoe-shiner. www.streetshine.com

MARK GRIFFITHS Mark is co-founder of Ideal Word, a values-led agency offering writing, brand language and corporate social responsibility (CSR) consultancy to clients including national and international brands, not-for-profit organisations and other creative agencies, from design to PR and internal communications. A published author, Mark runs Ideal Word with his wife, Debbie, to 'make words count' by helping organisations shape and communicate their image, ideas and ideals in words. www.idealword.co.uk

MILES HANSON Miles founded the Collaboration Company after a career in marketing. Miles believes in the power of collaboration to solve longstanding problems or strategic challenges and has developed his own method, which he calls Active Collaboration. He now works with a number of leading UK companies and charities. www.collaborationcompany.com

ROB HARRIS Rob is the founding Director of Advocacy Experience, which provides advocacy services to people with mental health problems and learning disabilities in the north-west of England.

OWEN JARVIS Owen founded the Cambridge branch of Aspire in the early 2000s then moved onto CAN to manage the Beanstalk social franchising programme. He is now Managing Director of Aspire Support UK, which is supporting new entrepreneurs working in the homelessness sector. www.aspire-support.co.uk

PHIL KNIBB Phil was one of the founder members of the 'Communiversity' in Croxteth, Liverpool, and is now Director of Alt Valley Community Trust, a series of highly social businesses providing employment and regeneration in the Croxteth area. www.communiversity.co.uk

ELIZABETH LASKAR Elizabeth is a co-founder of the Ethical Fashion Forum, which is a network of organisations in the fashion industry seeking to raise awareness of the importance of ethical approaches to the manufacture, sourcing and selling of fashion items. www.ethicalfashionforum.com

KAREN MATTISON Karen is founder and CEO of Women Like Us, a specialist recruitment business that helps women with children to make the best choices for their working lives, and helps employers find experienced part-time staff. They do this by offering coaching and advice, and delivering bespoke recruitment and consultancy services, specialising in flexible working. www.womenlikeus.org.uk

SERVANE MOUAZAN In 2000, Servane founded Ogunte, a global social entrepreneurship network which has been promoting social innovation and active citizenship through the facilitation of ethical events, participative development programmes and leadership coaching. www.ogunte.com

Luljeta Nuzi Luljeta founded Shpresa, an organisation that would reach out to those in the East London Albanian community who were struggling in their new surroundings. It now provides education and training opportunities to Albanian immigrants all over the UK. Shpresa is the Albanian word for 'hope'. www.shpresaprogramme.com

Steve Ralf Steve founded Focus to Work, which targets people in deprived areas of Kent to develop their opportunities in life through access to a number of social enterprises, including a café and a construction skills company. www.focustowork.co.uk

Bob Rhodes Bob was founder of TACT, a charity and social business that helps people with marked learning disabilities and very challenging reputations to pursue ordinary and less service-dependent lives in the community. Bob was Ernst and Young Social Entrepreneur of the Year in 2003. www.tactltd.org

Tom Savage Tom is a serial social entrepreneur, having set up three successful social enterprises by the age of 27. His latest is Bright Green Talent, whose mission is to identify and develop the talent to shape a better world. The company does this by helping organisations with an environmental or CSR agenda to recruit and retain the best people. www.brightgreentalent.com

Stephen Sears Stephen was one of the first members of staff of ECT Group, a community transport organisation in Ealing during the early 1980s. Today ECT Group is one of the largest social businesses in the UK, with major interests ranging from doorstep recycling to public transport. Stephen has been CEO now for over 20 years. www.ectgroup.co.uk

Jonathan Senker Jonathan joined Advocacy Partners when it was still a small organisation and has since grown it into one of the UK's leading providers of advocacy services to people with disabilities. www.advocacypartners.org

Shagufta Shahin Shagufta was a key player in building up an outstanding adult and community studies department at Barnfield College, an innovative higher education establishment in Luton. She is now Head of Foundation Studies at Newham College in London. www.barnfield.ac.uk

Julie Stokes OBE Julie is the founder of Winston's Wish, a charity that supports children who have been bereaved. Their service model has been used and adapted by many other organisations throughout the UK. www.winstonswish.org.uk

Nick Temple Nick is Network Director at the School for Social Entrepreneurs in Bethnal Green, which provides support for emerging entrepreneurial talent across the UK. He has previously run a number of social businesses himself. www.sse.org.uk

TIM WEST Tim is the founding editor of *Social Enterprise Magazine*, now the leading publication within the emerging social enterprise sector. He is also co-director of Society Media, a communications agency working with organisations from all sectors who are passionate about social change. www.socialenterprisemag.co.uk; www.societymedia.co.uk

HEATHER WILKINSON Heather founded Striding Out in order to provide support to younger social entrepreneurs. Striding Out offers coaching, networking, learning opportunities and professional advice to new social entrepreneurs. www.stridingout.co.uk

ROGER WILSON-HINDS Roger is the founder of Screenreader.net CIC Community Interest Company), which offers free software enabling blind people anywhere in the world to read the content of their computer screen. www.screenreader.net

About the author

Craig was born and brought up near Manchester. He studied Politics at the University of Newcastle. He then did two years of voluntary work in the North East before moving to Cambridge to take a job with a national charity. It was here that he founded Speaking Up as a 25-year-old. After two years he gave up his paid job to develop the organisation full time. That was over a decade ago. Speaking Up now supports 4,000 people each year, employs 100 people (one quarter of whom have disabilities or are former mental health service  users), works in 18 locations around the UK and has an annual financial turnover of over £3 million.

In 2006, Speaking Up won the Charity Award for Disability, a Third Sector Excellence Award, a Queen's Award for Voluntary Service and a Community Care Award for Learning Disabilities. In the last decade Craig has also co-founded several other social purpose organisations, most of which still exist.

He writes a monthly column for *Social Enterprise Magazine* and is a regular speaker at conferences and events. He now holds an MBA from the Open University and serves as a Social Enterprise Ambassador. Craig lives in Suffolk with his young family, is a passionate amateur runner and occasional triathlete.

To contact Craig go to www.craigdeardenphillips.com

What they said about the book...

'Craig's book gives an honest and frank account of what it takes to develop and run a social enterprise. I found myself smiling as each chapter reminded me of the highs and lows of setting up and running Unique. Its a great source of advice for anyone starting out, but also a really useful reminder to the veteran social entrepreneur that you are not alone!'

Matt Stevenson-Dodd
Chief Executive, Unique Social Enterprise CIC
Social Enterprise Ambassador

'The most practical, usable guide for social entrepreneurs I've read. Perfect for budding changemakers, because it's written by one.'

Nick Temple
Network Director, School for Social Entrepreneurs

'Social entrepreneurs are at the heart of social change in our country. I welcome this book as a new resource that will inspire and inform them.'

Phil Hope
MP, Minister for the Third Sector

Foreword

by Tim Smit CBE, Chief Executive of the Eden Project

We are living in fast-changing times. Whenever I talk to corporates, the message I get back is deafening: many of their brightest and best are now saying that money is not enough. It is my view that the role of the social entrepreneur is to create 'added value' to a wider definition than the company's financial bottom line.

To be clear about this, at a cost of £130 million the Eden Project would never have been able to turn a profit as a straight 'bottom line' business at all. However, over six years of operating it has been independently assessed as creating net wealth of nearly £1 billion.

The state should bite your arm off for such a result, but it is currently impossible to account in this way and so change patterns of capital investment.

The challenge for social enterprise is to come up with organisational models that are more sophisticated than not-for-profits, that adequately regard entrepreneurial spirit and risk-taking yet create a wider framework of value and have ethics running through them like Brighton through rock. Craig Dearden-Phillips is up for the challenge. Are you?

Social entrepreneurs need to think big because some of the major openings in future business will be on a massive scale. Global companies will be required to solve global problems. If we allow social enterprise to be pigeon-holed as 'not-real business' or viewed as part of the not-for-profit sector, we will have missed a golden opportunity. Because profit is not bad. Personal wealth is not bad. Being big is not bad. Unethical trading, pointless waste and missed opportunities to change the world – these are the things that are most definitely bad.

Social enterprise provides the mechanism for good business and good citizenship. For me, this looks like a roadmap to a contented future. And I suspect, the world might breathe a huge sigh of relief at the same time!

This book is about changing the world – and how to go about it. Through Eden we have done it one way and you may have seen the result. We started with a vision, powerful guiding values and a big hole in the ground that flooded in the winter. We didn't have a penny in the bank and everyone told us we couldn't do it. Everything starts in the mind. Every fire needs a spark. Craig's book will help turn sparks to flames. I commend it to you.

Introduction

Entrepreneurship is the last refuge of the trouble-making individual.
Natalie Clifford Barney, American poet and writer

This book is for people who are active social entrepreneurs or for those seriously considering jacking in the day-job to become one …

I've written it because I have been there and want to help others who are starting out. Ten years ago, support for emerging social entrepreneurs was non-existent. I wanted to write the book I never had when I began my own journey. The book that tells you some of the things that you really need to know. The book that brings together the experience of a whole bunch of other people who have been there themselves.

My belief in social entrepreneurship comes from my conviction about the special role that individuals play in changing the world for the better. History has produced an amazing number of social entrepreneurs, whose ideas and organisations have helped shape our world. Make no mistake: social entrepreneurs will matter in the future, too. Increasing numbers of people see that the world's challenges are too big for governments alone to sort out. New kinds of action and innovation are required. In the thick of all of this, social entrepreneurs from all sectors – private, public and voluntary – will forge new alliances and create new kinds of solutions.

Who are these people? Tens of thousands of social entrepreneurs operate worldwide, from well-known names like Tim Smit of the Eden Project through to the relatively unknown, like Doug Cresswell in Stockport, whose company, Pure Innovations, is changing the business model for learning disability services. In this book I speak to 25 social entrepreneurs. These people are mostly, but not all, founders of their organisations. Some joined a little way in, like Hannah Eyres of Keyfund and Jonathan Senker of Advocacy Partners. I deliberately picked a diverse group of people from a range of sectors and parts of the country. Some, like Julie Stokes of Winston's Wish, founded charities. Others, like Steve Ralf of Focus to Work, set up CICs. One or two, like Tom Savage of Bright Green Talent, actually own the businesses they founded. I also spoke to social business 'giants' like Steve Sears of ECT Group (with a turnover of tens of millions of pounds) as well as newcomers, such as Roger Wilson-Hinds of Screenreader, a two-person business.

A few of the people featured here are becoming well-known names but many will, I hope, be new to you. It is crucial, I believe, that less well-known voices are heard in a sector that can appear to be dominated by a handful of 'celebrity' social entrepreneurs.

I also saw it as vital not to be picky about the type of organisation entrepreneurs come from, be it a charity, a CIC, a private company or the public sector. We are all social entrepreneurs if we think and act in a particular way. As Liam Black, Director of Fifteen, correctly points out, social enterprise is a 'state of mind' as much as a single organisational format.

What about me? I started my own journey 12 years ago when I was 25 years of age – I quit my job in a big national charity and I have dedicated my life since to building Speaking Up. We support people with disabilities so they can have a voice and control their own lives. Speaking Up now works with thousands of people each year, employs 100 people, around a quarter of whom have experience of disability or severe mental health problems. It has an annual turnover of £3 million (2007–8) and has won a clutch of big national awards. As a founder, I feel that, after a massive slog, my dreams are starting to be realised.

I have also been involved in founding a number of other new ventures as a director or trustee. Two of these new organisations were spin-offs from Speaking Up. The other three were brand-new ventures. Viewing these from the balcony, so to speak, has given me a wider view of the challenges facing any new business.

Not all of these organisations still exist. Although I have been successful at Speaking Up, my track record is fairly mixed. Over the years, I have made as many mistakes as winning decisions. Sharing these – and the learning that came out of them – is one of my main goals in writing this book.

I know you won't have a lot of time, so this book is designed to be dipped into when you need to. The book focuses on your first few years in business. Whether you are setting up a new charity or a social business, the book is designed to be a companion to you on that journey. I have tried to make it straightforward to read and full of ideas and tips rather than exhaustive detail.

This book is also designed to make you think. I don't actually believe that reading books by itself really helps you learn. But *grappling* with a book is a completely different matter. For this reason, this book frequently asks you to think hard and jot down your thoughts. The more you do this, the more you'll get out of it.

Finally, you may be asking yourself, 'Am I a social entrepreneur?' Well, there are long and often very boring debates about the nature of social entrepreneurs – normally conducted by people with the time and energy to ruminate on these things. My advice is not to worry too much about whether you are or not. The key thing about you, which makes you different from most other people, is that you want to act to create social change. This is what matters more than anything else. You may have a new approach to an old problem. Or you could be up-scaling a small idea that's worked well locally, or be adopting a brilliant idea you've seen somewhere else. You may not necessarily be a founder; you may have arrived a little way in. You may be setting up a new charity or thinking of running your own business. It really doesn't matter how you do it. What is most important is *what* you do. If you are seriously committed to changing the world, this is definitely a book for you. Enjoy.

Craig Dearden-Phillips
January 2008

1 Is this for you? The social entrepreneur's journey

The greatest mystery of life, is who we truly are.
Alexandre Dumas, French novelist and playwright
(1802–1870)

'Is this for you?' Only by answering this question honestly can you really go ahead. The demands of social entrepreneurship are such that you've got to really want to do it. I mean *really* want to do it. For you're not only giving up a job, assuming you have one, you're also giving up a lifestyle – that of the employee and regular person.

Instead, you're looking at long hours and putting the rest of your life on hold for at least a couple of years until your venture is established. All in pursuit of a cause you believe in. In short, the list of sacrifices is long and the risks, particularly to your reputation, are high. You'll live with uncertainty and total responsibility for your venture. There will be no safety net. So, ask yourself, 'Is this for me?' Remember, it is much braver to admit it isn't than push ahead with something when you're less than 100% sure of your desire. If you're in any doubt about your desire, I would say 'hold back for now'. The challenges ahead can only be tackled from a position of total commitment.

What's your motivation?

I wanted to be an editor or a journalist, I wasn't really interested in being an entrepreneur, but I soon found I had to become an entrepreneur in order to keep my magazine going.
Sir Richard Branson, founder of Virgin

So before you start, it is worth getting one thing clear: '*Why* do I want to do this?' A study into successful UK social entrepreneurs by Chambers and Edwards-Stuart (2007),[1] shows that social entrepreneurs see unmet need and feel compelled to do something. They are disillusioned with conventional approaches to problems and seek new solutions. But, unlike most people, social entrepreneurs act. What separates them from the crowd is that they have the drive and energy to start shaping up a practical response to the problem. The decision to act is emotional as much as intellectual. Drawing on the legend of King Arthur, the authors call this an 'Excalibur moment'.

Does this sound at all like you? Do you feel compelled to act? My Excalibur moment came when I arrived in Cambridge in my mid-twenties. I had just spent two years doing confidence-building work among learning-disabled adults in the north of England. This work had touched my heart. I had also been a care worker and seen with my own eyes what better lives people had

---

[1] Charlotte Chambers and Fiona Edwards-Stuart (2007), 'Leadership in the Social Economy', School for Social Entrepreneurs.

when they were supported in making choices. I knew from then that my long-term future lay in supporting people to have a voice and gain control of their own lives. To my surprise, when I arrived, nothing like this existed in Cambridgeshire. I made a snap decision: I would make it happen.

Then the real work began. In my spare time, I started to network locally and develop the early organisation. This was well before I quit my job to develop the organisation full time. My motivation was a realisation that if I didn't do this, no-one else would. I knew that if I could pull it off, Speaking Up would be, in a sense, my personal contribution. I sensed too, in quite an overwhelming way, that this was my life's work, what I was here to do.

What followed were probably the hardest five years of my life – hardest because I made some horrendous mistakes. Hardest because I worked like a horse, surviving on Silk Cut, Pot Noodles and Red Bull.

But it was also the best. Best because the sheer thrill of developing a successful new organisation has to rank as one of the best there is. Best because I saw life-transforming changes in the people with whom we worked. Best because of the pure joy of building something in which we all believed.

I know I'm not alone in feeling this way. When I asked a group of social entrepreneurs for their best and worst experiences, their answers seemed very familiar to me. Steve Ralf of Focus to Work told me that, 'The reward of seeing change in people on a daily basis is the best. The worst is the long hours and poor work/life balance.' The comments of TACT's Bob Rhodes seemed to echo this: 'The best include freedom to express oneself, create and make a big difference; the worst is the impact of this over-riding obsession on those you love. Later it can be managed but in the early years long hours and total focus seem to be unavoidable.'

Karen Mattison of Women Like Us told me a story about watching a woman who had been low in confidence, isolated and desperate for some local part-time work actually get a great job that she could fit around her children. 'Watching her transformation makes everything worthwhile.'

For Tim West of *Social Enterprise Magazine*, 'Best: freedom to take risks. Worst: freedom to take risks.' It's a similar feeling for Stephen Sears of the ECT Group: 'The best thing is the freedom, the worst is the insecurity – you can't have one without the other.'

Views from the social entrepreneurs

Why did you take the plunge and set up on your own?

- 'It's the attraction of feeling like a pioneer in a new land, doing something new, setting your own course while doing things you feel passionately about.' (Owen Jarvis, Aspire Support UK)

- 'The time had come to be free from the constraints of local authority systems and controls as they had started to hinder development and delivery rather than help.' (Doug Cresswell, Pure Innovations)

- 'An overwhelming need that felt difficult to ignore.' (Julie Stokes, Winston's Wish)

- 'I felt compelled to share the freedom and empowerment our talking software has given us with others who can't see.' (Roger Wilson-Hinds, Screenreader)

- 'Because I was so frustrated at not being able to get anything done in a charity and any decision made by a local authority.' (Steve Ralf, Focus to Work)

In my experience, the 'bests' outnumber the 'worsts'. But each 'best' and 'worst' is an extreme. Life as a social entrepreneur feels much more intense than life when you're doing a 'normal' job. The best bits of becoming a social entrepreneur will surpass anything you have ever experienced at work. Equally, the worst bits are truly dreadful. I remember, many times, opening envelopes thinking 'If this isn't good news, we are finished'. Jobs lost, three years of my life down the drain. People saying 'Told you so!'

What are the common features of successful social entrepreneurs?

> *Life is either a daring adventure or nothing.*
> *Helen Keller, deaf-blind American author*

What do successful social entrepreneurs look like? While they come in all shapes and sizes there is, I believe, a 'DNA' (albeit one that can be acquired!) that all successful social entrepreneurs possess. I agree strongly with Chambers and Edwards-Stuart's work on this. Interestingly, all these traits have a potential downside, too. Here is a summary of these traits:

1. They use their gut as much as their brain
Upside: social entrepreneurs tend to be intuitive rather than analytical. They 'feel' as much as 'think' when making decisions. They are imaginative, good at seeing trends and painting pictures of the future. When they get it right, social entrepreneurs can generate solutions that are fresh and compelling.

Downside: they are prone to building 'castles in the air', which stay there if they don't have the ability to follow through.

2. They have unusual drive

Upside: social entrepreneurs have a high drive for achievement. This is grounded either in their personal 'Excalibur moment' or something in their own background. It gives them the will to overcome huge hurdles and persist long after many would have given up.

Downside: channelled the wrong way, this drive can lead to tunnel vision and rigid thinking that stops them adapting to new circumstances.

3. They possess powerful values

Upside: successful people in social enterprise are highly principled, have a strong internal moral compass that guides them and an ability to embed these values into an organisation.

Downside: some people let their principles lead them to decisions that feel morally right but in fact lead to the demise of their organisation – and its good work.

4. They have strong focus

Upside: social entrepreneurs are able to settle on a handful of big-ticket goals the short and medium terms while also keeping in mind the long-term horizon.

Downside: an inability to retune their radar to new and shifting situations.

5. They are full of self-confidence

Upside: social entrepreneurs display high levels of self-belief. They are aware of their own strengths and are realistic, too, about their limitations. This self-belief is particularly helpful in securing early support.

Downside: played the wrong way, the sense of self can result in the organisation appearing to be an extension of the social entrepreneur's ego.

6. They have fantastic communication skills

Upside: social entrepreneurs tend to be affable and charming communicators who can adapt themselves to working with people from all walks of life.

Downside: they can appear to be insubstantial in character and, in the words of one of my own staff when she first met me, 'all charm, no trousers' …

7. They have good emotional intelligence

Upside: social entrepreneurs are excellent at assessing the emotional needs and potential contributions of key players. They are emotionally intelligent people who connect with people's core values. They have the people skills to build the necessary coalitions to take a venture to its next stage.

Downside: social entrepreneurs can come across as overwhelming and too single-minded – which can be a turn-off.

8. They have first-class networking skills

Upside: successful social entrepreneurs are consummate networkers. They are alive to the potential of every contact and use networking in a strategic way to scan the horizon, line up allies and understand the political landscape. They are particularly skilled at linking people together from different parts of their network to create new possibilities.

Downside: they can potentially be chameleon-like, appealing to every network for strategic reasons but not always meaning it.

9. They value stewardship

Upside: really successful social entrepreneurs view themselves as stewards, not owners, of an organisation.

Downside: they may not recognise that, while their personal contribution will always be important, it is equally vital that they either change with the organisation or prepare it for their departure.

10. They are natural leaders

Upside: successful social entrepreneurs are good at creating an exciting and energetic atmosphere in the workplace. They are, on the whole, good people-managers and understand the importance of a positive organisational culture.

Downside: they need to take care not to create a 'cult of personality' around themselves, which results in the organisation falling over when they leave.

Does any of this sound like you? Upsides or downsides? If you're planning to become a social entrepreneur, it is worth gauging yourself honestly against this list – or asking somebody to do it with you.

The people I interviewed for this book have some interesting views about what makes for a successful social entrepreneur. Miles Hanson said it was about 'real belief in their idea, no fear of selling and a good business mind'. On a similar note, Tom Savage of Bright Green Talent believes that 'successful entrepreneurs have a willingness to constantly improve themselves'. Nick Temple of School for Social Entrepreneurs points to 'vision, passion, persistence, pragmatism, relationship-building and self-awareness', while Luljeta Nuzi of Shpresa simply says that the very best social entrepreneurs 'don't take no for an answer'.

Born or made?

> *Nobody talks of entrepreneurship as survival, but that's exactly what it is and what nurtures creative thinking.*
> *Dame Anita Roddick, founder of The Body Shop*

While there are *born* social entrepreneurs – this doesn't mean they cannot be *made*. I certainly don't see myself as a born entrepreneur. For every story of a lifelong social entrepreneur who has been leading since they were in the playground, there are many more for whom social entrepreneurship has been a response to the world as they have found it, rather than an inborn drive or predisposition.

It is clear from the lives of the people I know that social entrepreneurs are often made as much as born. Many spent years in futile, pointless jobs before starting up. Several, like Roger Wilson-Hinds of Screenreader, came to it later in life. For some, including myself, social entrepreneurship was the only option if they wanted to achieve particular social goals.

I see myself as something of an accidental entrepreneur – made more than born. I happened upon entrepreneurship through my social passion, not the other way round. And at no stage did anyone view me as remotely entrepreneurial as I was growing up – neither driven, nor a consummate networker. All these traits followed the development of my social mission. Some of them I had to learn, such as the ability to build networks and sell what I was doing. Others came more naturally

So when you read these long lists of what makes a great social entrepreneur, don't necessarily measure yourself against the person you have been up until now; nor against those who have already been successful. Instead ask yourself, could you *become* a social entrepreneur, if doing so helped you to pursue your social mission?

The four phases of life for a social enterprise

> *I lead my life by two theories: 'Tinkerbell', which holds that if you can get enough people to believe in something it will almost certainly happen, and 'Last Man Standing', which says that if you have a degree of charm and people know you won't go away, they will eventually pay you to do so.*
>
> Tim Smit, founder of the Eden Project

So what are you letting yourself in for? Your new venture will have a life cycle of four phases that it will inevitably go through. This book covers all of these, from conception right up to the point where you want to seriously grow and replicate your venture.

The four phases, adapted from Chambers and Edwards-Stuart, cover dreaming, acting, sustaining and scaling. Let me briefly take you through each.

Phase 1 – dreaming
This is the reflective period you're in now or were in not so long ago. You are getting together your ideas, researching the area, talking to a lot of different people, scoping approaches and working out a new 'space' you could move into. This is a time when the problem crystallises into a burning idea for a solution, something you find so compelling that you have to act.

Phase 2 – acting

This is the frenetic year or two during which you'll be multi-tasking and developing contacts at a rapid rate. You'll be developing your supporter or customer base, experimenting with your business model and getting some very basic structures and processes into place. In a typical day, you'll be engaged in every area of the organisation and having the time of your life – in every possible sense. At the end of this phase you'll have refined your vision, found some customers or users and secured the resources to develop to the next phase.

Phase 3 – sustaining

This often comes after a couple of years. It involves building a solid infrastructure, and developing robust organisational systems and processes. This is where the pairing between you as social entrepreneur and a new recruit with stronger managerial skills becomes important. This is the part of the journey where you start to create a full-blown organisation and a proper team to take forward your vision. It is also, inevitably, a period when you will experience challenges concerning financial stability, governance and sustainability. Crucially, this is a time that many social entrepreneurs find difficult. Often there is a need to modify goals, revamp methods and accept new ways of doing things. This can feel like a betrayal of earlier times. Many social entrepreneurs start to think about how their venture might up-scale – or replicate. Many in the thick of all of this decide now to quit and hand the organisation over to somebody else …

Phase 4 – scaling

This is also a difficult phase, one at which many social entrepreneurs start to encounter real problems. These arise, firstly, from the inherent challenge of up-scaling a business – finding finance, developing the organisation, maintaining the culture. Many social entrepreneurs experience difficulty in adapting to the new requirements of leading as a CEO. For this reason, this is often the hopping-off point for many. The truth of the matter may be that the personal style, skill set and aptitude of the entrepreneur is not well suited to the demands of a growing company. However, this doesn't mean an entrepreneur has to quit. Many choose to upgrade their skills and stay. Faced with the challenge of growth, I decided to do an MBA and develop myself into a manager. But this phase does require the entrepreneur to make a big decision: to stay – and change – or to go.

What will it take to be successful?

The upside-down pyramid for getting rich

1. Commit or don't commit. No half-measures
2. Cut loose from all negative influences
3. Choose the right mountain
4. Fear nothing
5. Start now
6. Go

Felix Dennis, UK publishing magnate

Unlike Felix Dennis, you're probably not trying to get seriously rich, but you certainly want to succeed. In this respect, his advice is pretty near the mark. So too is what you'll hear from the social entrepreneurs interviewed as part of this book. All have built their organisations to at least phase 3, sustaining, and many into phase 4, scaling, so it is worth listening carefully to what they have to say. Their messages, while all different, do provide clear pointers. I'll finish this chapter where I started, with another important question.

IS THIS FOR YOU?

Has this chapter been useful for you?
Are you clearer about whether this is a journey you want to take?

- If this is not for you, there is no shame in your decision – becoming a social entrepreneur is no worthier a role in life than becoming a brilliant teacher, nurse or architect.
- If this is for you, it's important that you're resourced and supported to do it.
- If this is for you, prepare for the time of your life!

Given a big enough 'why', people can bear almost any 'how'.
Friedrich Nietzsche, German philosopher

2 Is this a runner?

You have 50,000 thoughts a day, you might as well make them big ones.
Donald Trump, American billionaire

Before you even start to plan your venture in detail, you need to ask yourself whether your idea has 'legs'. There is some hard thinking to do before you invest lots of time and energy into something. Ask yourself:

- What will my business do?
- How will it operate?
- Who will be my customers?
- How would I explain my business idea to a seven-year-old child?
- What is the long-term purpose of this business?
- What would amazing success look like?
- Why do I want to create this business?
- What would I like to be celebrating this time next year?
- What will my business be known for?
- If everything went to plan, what would the business look like in five years' time?
- What will make my business succeed?

Whether you are planning to run a community café employing former drug users or hoping to sell bottled water in order to give away your profits, you'll need to think all of these points through in a hard-headed way.

You won't get a final answer – who ever knows for sure whether their idea will succeed? But you will have gone through an important process that will increase your odds of success. Indeed, had I asked some of these questions earlier in my ventures I may have spared myself the pain of setting up organisations that eventually failed!

What will be your offer?

I find out what the world needs then I proceed to invent it.
Thomas Edison, inventor of the light bulb

Every new charity or business needs to solve a problem. Therefore, the key question facing a new venture is 'Where's the pain?' To get you thinking about your own future business, have a go now at answering these questions:

- What problem are you trying to solve?
- Who, in precise terms, are you seeking to help?
- Could you write a short description of the typical person you're trying to help?

- What does the latest research on this problem tell you?
- What are the big trends that are affecting the area you plan to work in?
- What is distinctive or new about your approach to this problem?
- Which agencies will you be working with to solve the problem?
- What 'business model' could you use to tackle the problem and guarantee an income at the same time?

Answering these questions successfully will enable you to get a clear idea of what you could do and who might be out there to pay for it.

The people I interviewed for this book had clear ideas from the outset. For Elizabeth Laskar, of the Ethical Fashion Forum, it was 'a passion to do something about the social and environmental impact of the fashion sector'. For Julie Stokes of Winston's Wish, the purpose was to support bereaved children whose needs were not met by the NHS. But crucially, all had also worked out possible ways to turn their vision into a viable organisation.

Who will pay for what you do?

The million dollar question. For ordinary businesses, this is normally the end customers, the person who buys their product. This is the same for many social businesses too. Indeed some, like Steve Sears' ECT Group, operate in very tough markets dominated by big private contractors and rely for most of their income on being the best in the business. The main visible difference between these social enterprises and private ones is that social business processes are designed to produce social benefits as well as profit. And, of course, profits are used for social good rather than being given back to shareholders. But the basis of commercial success for social businesses like ECT Group is the same as it is for any business: sell lots of stuff to lots of people at a profit. For these companies, social enterprise is simply 'business for a social purpose'.

However, selling lots of stuff isn't always possible. This is why some social entrepreneurs have to take a different approach to their core purpose. Many social entrepreneurs work, particularly early on, in the context of total market failure. I was one of them, at first. To address market failures these entrepreneurs often need grants and donations before establishing a more stable funding arrangement. Like Julie Stokes. She was working with bereaved children and it took her some time to get the organisation onto a stable financial footing.

For these entrepreneurs – and you may become one of them – the question of 'Who pays?' is always more complex than selling lots of stuff. In fact, you may have to admit, right from the start, that your venture will never be sustained by sales alone. Sales may form part of your income but there may always be a big element of grant funding. This is certainly the case for Speaking Up. It is better to admit this early on than pretend that you can earn all the cash you need from sales or contracts. Although some would disagree, I don't believe this makes you any less of a social entrepreneur.

So the main question facing you as a social entrepreneur doesn't have to be, 'How can I become self-sustaining without grants?' While for some this will be a definite aim, it just isn't realistic for many others. Instead, the real question you need to ask is, 'Can I find the income I need to achieve my social purposes?' If you can obtain 'free money' in the form of grants or donations, then as long as you can prove you are adding an equivalent in social value, then you should not, as a social entrepreneur, have any big worries about this. We all do it. In fact, I don't know of many social enterprises where 'free money' – which is all grants are – do not form at least part of the organisation's income. Even the big social enterprise success-stories we hear about all the time get some 'free money'. The key thing for you to work out isn't how to turn what you are doing into a conventional business but how you can find long-term sources of income.

> *The key thing for you to work out isn't how to turn what you are doing into a conventional business but how you can find long-term sources of income.*

I asked my panel of social entrepreneurs for their views on what people need to think about most when they are starting out. Their answers are varied and revealing. For Karen Mattison, sustainability is important. 'Can it make money and be self-sustaining?' are the key questions she believes you should ask. Phil Knibb of Alt Valley Community Trust urges you to ask, 'Is what you are doing going to improve people's quality of life? Or are you just doing something cheaper than some other business?' While Heather Wilkinson of Striding Out suggests you ask yourself 'where the finance is going to come from to cover start-up costs and how future income is going to be generated.'

What's the competition?

> *All is theft, all is unceasing and rigorous competition in nature; the desire to make off with the substance of others is the foremost, the most legitimate passion nature has bred into us and, without doubt, the most agreeable one.*
>
> Marquis de Sade, French aristocrat and writer

Even if your view of human nature is a little more positive than that of the Marquis de Sade, you will face ferocious competition in the social enterprise sector. Please have no illusions about this. If you are a market-based social enterprise, you will face stiff competition from commercial operators who won't care if you're trying to do good stuff on top of building a strong business. If you are working in the voluntary sector, the competition is probably even more extreme. There is far more need than there are resources available. The sheer number of organisations now competing for funding is more than at any other point in history – about 170,000 charities plus hundreds of cash-hungry new CICs.

As a new organisation, you face the disadvantage, too, of being unknown. Unlike the big-name organisations, you have no brand, track record or reputation. For this reason, you need to be better than the competition in some key ways if you are going to succeed.

Your competitor analysis needs to start with a frank assessment of the sector you are in and the other organisations working there. Although you may, in the future, work in partnership with some of these agencies, they are, in a very real sense, your competitors. This is because they will currently have customers you want for yourself or investment income that you need to get your hands on.

In the early days of Speaking Up, we had three main sets of competitors. The first were the well-known disability charities, which we felt had failed people so badly in the past. The second were small local organisations competing with us for funding. The third were statutory agencies, which tended to monopolise public funding for their own programmes.

We felt we had the following advantages over our competitors:
- **Freshness** – We were fresh and modern in our outlook compared to the dreary, grey charities that seemed to dominate the disability world.
- **Entrepreneurialism** – We had an entrepreneurial attitude and moved quickly, unlike other organisations, which seemed slow and conservative.
- **Involvement** – We had disabled people personally involved at all levels, which gave us huge credibility among disabled people.

Thinking now about your new venture, who do you see as your potential competitors?

The next step is to conduct a methodical analysis of your competitors' strengths and weaknesses. Why is this important? The writer Robert M. Grant[1] contends that a company succeeds through the assets, skills and competitive advantages that it brings into the marketplace. Success is about your strengths as an organisation as much as the gaps in the market. An analysis of competitors who are currently successful should reveal what it takes to succeed in your sector. Try to do the exercise below.

Analyse the competition			
Competitor	**What are their competitive advantages?**	**What are their competitive weaknesses?**	**How can you compete with them?**

[1] Robert M. Grant (2004), *Contemporary Strategy Analysis*, Blackwell.

Business model

Wealth is the product of man's ability to think.

Ayn Rand, novelist and philosopher

What is a business model? Your business model defines how you approach a problem. It is simply an explanation of your operation and states; in precise terms, how you propose to go about tackling the issue you've identified. A new venture normally proposes a new business model. Your business model tells someone what is distinctive about your approach and what it costs to do it your way. I will use Speaking Up as an example:

The Speaking Up business model is to gain funding from a third party (often a local authority or healthcare organisation) to work intensively alongside individuals on a short-term basis so that they have a voice and can gain control over key areas of their lives. Our involvement is normally fairly short term but high impact. We work on a specific issue, or set of issues, and exit once the issue is dealt with.

Try now (I suggest on a flip chart) to answer the questions below about your own business model.

Identify your business model

- Why will people come to us?
- How will people enter or access our service?
- What will we do for them?
- How long will we work with them?
- What will our service feel like to people using it?
- What kind of evidence will we have of success?
- What will be the cost per beneficiary?
- Who will pay this bill?

Why will you succeed?

A business is successful to the extent that it provides a product or service that contributes to happiness in all of its forms.

Mihaly Csikszentmihalyi, American author

Successful organisations get things right that others don't. You need to be clear about the ways in which you're going to try to out-perform the others. For some businesses, their advantage is price – they try to be cheaper than everyone else. For others, it's about a clever new way of delivering something that is new and that people will like. For most, however, it is about delivering a better service – being more relevant to need; being liked by your customers, whoever they are. Really successful organisations manage all of these things. But not many. Normally, it is about finding one, maybe two areas of advantage. You need to think long and hard, 'Why will I succeed'?

The success of Speaking Up to date is, I believe, down to two or three things. Firstly, we have been good at creating new answers to old questions – or innovation. Secondly, we have worked hard at developing first-class relationships with all our clients and customers. We try hard to be enjoyable to deal with and to be liked. Finally, we push very hard to deliver quality in our services and put our energy into this before our internal issues.

All of these positives reflect early decisions we made about how we would forge success: we would be innovative, we would seek to be the best in delivery and we would be great to work with. We knew that in a sector with plenty of conservative, low-quality, unpopular organisations, we had a chance of success by doing this.

IS THIS A RUNNER?

Has this chapter been useful for you?
Do you think you have something you can take forward?

- Thinking now about the viability of your idea may save you some painful learning down the line.
- How you will resource your dream is something you must have ideas about before you start.
- You need to have defined your offer, understood your competition and figured out some way of operating, however basic.
- Be clear about why you will succeed – it will be very tough out there!

Whatever you can do or dream you can begin it. Boldness has genius, power and magic in it.

Johann Wolfgang von Goethe, German poet

3 Off the back of the envelope: your first business plan

First, have a definite, clear practical ideal: a goal, an objective. Second, have the necessary means to achieve your ends: wisdom, money, materials, and methods. Third, adjust all your means to that end.

Aristotle, Ancient Greek scientist and philosopher

Among his many achievements, Aristotle was also one of the earliest social entrepreneurs, founding a school of philosophy, the Lyceum. Aristotle lived nearly two and half thousand years ago, but his words are as true today for people with big dreams as they were in ancient Athens.

Aristotle was talking about the importance of having a good strategy. But don't his words seem rather *obvious*? Any trawl of the Internet or business textbook will tell you the same thing in a thousand different ways.

However, by and large, people fail to identify clear goals and work to a plan. Instead, they muddle along. But, if you follow Aristotle's advice and plan your new venture properly, you'll be one of the few who actually succeed as a social entrepreneur.

In my view, the very act of writing a business plan immediately boosts your chances of success. If you are in any doubt, ask anyone who has actually succeeded. Of the six start-ups I've been involved with, three had decent business plans and three didn't. You can guess which ones still exist.

A business plan answers all the big questions facing your new venture. These include:

- What is the vision of the future you're working towards?
- What is the purpose or mission of your new venture?
- Where's the pain, or who will your new venture help'?
- Who else is in your field competing with you?
- What is your business model (or particular approach to helping people)?
- What will the venture actually look like once it's working?
- What is your budget for the first three years?
- How will the venture survive and grow?
- Why should you receive financial backing?

A business plan has many purposes. For you it is a planning tool and a check on how you are doing. For those around you, it should be a source of inspiration and give clarity of purpose. For investors and funders, it should give them the information they need to make a decision to back you. In short, it must convince.

Start with the end in mind – capturing your vision, mission and goals

One person with passion is better than forty people merely interested.
> E.M. Forster, English novelist

How do you go about planning for the future? The people I interviewed about this book are quite clear. 'By setting simple, easy-to-grasp strategic priorities', says Richard Alderson of Careershifters. For Mark Griffiths, of Ideal Word, 'It's necessary to have different future visions and remind yourselves of them constantly – a long-term dream; a mid-term position that you're prepared to accept; some short-term goals that you really need to focus on if you are even to have a future.'

In the first part of this section, we look at vision, mission and goals. These are the key building blocks of your first business plan. Then we look at the other components of the plan: market analysis, competitor analysis, business model, budget and executive summary.

We'll cover what needs to be in there, what you can leave out, how it should look and read and how to make the business plan a living document. Throughout the chapter, I'll ask you to think about the big questions and jot down your answers. By the end, you should be in a position to write your business plan.

There are lots of ways of doing business plans but the structure outlined here is the most powerful. Ideally, your plan should be no more than 20 pages long. It should be short and to the point. By all means include some drawings, graphs and photos, but don't over-do them. People need to 'get' the plan immediately. If they don't, you're never going to get out of the starting blocks.

Vision

Vision is the art of seeing things invisible.
> Jonathan Swift, Irish poet

Creating a vision is one of the earliest and most important tasks for the social entrepreneur. A vision is quite literally a picture of an ideal future. The power of your vision will have a big effect on everyone involved in your venture. A vision is always inspiring and idealistic, but also achievable.

Some of the best-known statements of organisational vision have actually come from business entrepreneurs. Back in the 1970s, Bill Gates, founder of Microsoft, created this vision statement for his company: 'A personal computer in every home running Microsoft software'.

At the time, Gates' vision seemed extraordinary. Most people hadn't come across computers, except perhaps huge 'mainframes' at work. But for Gates, the vision of mass computer ownership became the driving force of his company and an important factor in its eventual success.

As a social entrepreneur, your own vision will probably extend beyond your own organisation to reflect the kind of world you're seeking to create. What is your social vision? Write it down!

My own vision developed in my twenties in response to what I found out about the lives of people with learning difficulties. I encountered beautiful young women who were forced to have hysterectomies at 16. I met grown men in their forties who were paid £2 a week to pack soap in a day centre. I felt upset and angry. To turn this into something positive, I developed a vision of a society in which learning-disabled people enjoyed comparable lives to people without disabilities.

My social vision led me to plan Speaking Up as a different type of disability organisation. I wanted an equal partnership between disabled people and their allies and an organisation that gave people the capacity to take control of their own lives.

The power of visualisation

The more intensely we feel about an idea or a goal, the more assuredly the idea, buried deep in our subconscious, will direct us along the path to its fulfillment.

Earl Nightingale, American writer and broadcaster

When you speak to successful people from any walk of life you will often find that they had, from a very early stage, a powerful mental image of what the future would look like.

Visualisation is a technique used very commonly in professional sport and now increasingly used in other settings. It involves imagining, in a very specific way, what success looks and feels like. The idea is that once you've visualised success, your unconscious mind will help you to achieve it.

I have used visualisation all my life. I use it to imagine success. Early on, just as I was starting out, I created a mental picture of Speaking Up ten years in. I am totally convinced that my early visualisation has helped to succeed in building my organisation to where it is today.

Visualise your success

Close your eyes for a few moments and think about the following questions. After a while, open your eyes and write down what you saw.

In three years from now:

My new venture will be creating this social vision by _____ .

We will be working with _____ people.

We will have made a difference by _____ .

We will have succeeded because _____ .

My role will have been to _____ .

Mission

Things do not happen. Things are made to happen.
> John F. Kennedy, US President 1960–63

A mission statement is a declaration of what, in concrete terms, a new venture aspires to achieve. If your vision answers the question 'What?', your mission statement answers the question 'How?' The mission statement is the business' proclamation of why it exists, a clarification of who it serves, and an expression of what it hopes to achieve in the future.

The process of writing a mission statement helps a new or established business to clarify questions such as:

- What business are we really in?
- What type of business do we want to be?
- What is our target customer?
- What inspires us?

The writing process and the statement itself both provide clarity of purpose and motivation for business success.

Mission statement characteristics

A mission statement has the following key characteristics:

- **Aspirational** – Above all a mission statement articulates what your new venture aspires to become. It helps people understand what the business is about and how they can contribute to the achievement of the vision.
- **Broad** – A mission statement should be broad enough to allow the company to meet those needs without annual revisions of the statement.
- **Realistic** – A lofty, unrealistic mission statement will not have great credibility. Instead the best statements are direct and powerful.
- **Motivational** – The statement should be written in such a way that it inspires commitment from potential supporters and employees.
- **Short and concise** – The mission statement should be no longer than 30 words. It should certainly be short enough for an employee to remember it easily and repeat it readily. Management guru, Peter Drucker, suggests it should be able to fit on a t-shirt.
- **Easily understood** – The statement should use plain language that is convincing and easy to understand. Consider using the 'parents' test' on your mission statement – would your parents understand what your venture is about if they read your mission statement?

Here are a few very snappy mission statements from a range of organisations you may have heard about:

Google – *'Organise the world's information and make it universally accessible and useful.'*

PEPSI – *'Beat Coke.'*

Walt Disney – *'To make people happy.'*

UN High Commission for Human Rights – *'To protect and promote all human rights for all.'*

National Council of Voluntary Organisations (NCVO) – *'A vibrant voluntary and community sector deserves a strong voice and the best support. NCVO aims to be that support and voice.'*

The key test is for a mission statement to work even when you *haven't* heard of the organisation. Think for a second about your own venture, how could you find a way to make your mission similarly clear?

Some organisations use their mission statements, or a condensed version, as a strapline, often combining it with their logo or making it very clear on their website:

'Women Like Us – bringing women and employers together with flexible work.'

'Ideal Word – make words count.'

'Careershifters – get excited about your work.'

'Striding Out – supporting young people with enterprising ideas.'

'AspireSupportUK – creating real jobs for homeless people.'

Developing your elevator pitch

> *We'd love to be involved with the creation of something very special, something quite large and something quite exciting.*
> Sir Richard Branson, founder of Virgin

Imagine you're in a lift for 30 seconds with Richard Branson and he asks about your new venture. It's a brilliant test because you've got to get the essence of your mission across very quickly, in a way that anyone can understand.

I had my own Branson moment some years ago when I had a very short encounter with a wealthy person from the City. I was trying to get him interested in helping me up-scale Speaking Up. On that occasion I botched it. Here is what I said:

We work in the field of empowerment. I need help to disseminate our learning to other stakeholders in the disability sector so that we can remedy social exclusion experienced by this oppressed group. To do this we need core funding to build our organisational capacity.

The guy's face quickly glazed over; he hadn't understood a single word I had said. Thankfully, he quite liked me and agreed to meet again.

What was my mistake? I had made three big howlers. The first was to assume he knew something about my world. He didn't – any more than I knew about hedge funds. Secondly, I used language that may have impressed a room full of social workers but was no good for the average person. Finally, I failed to engage him emotionally. I didn't convey how we changed people's lives.

At our next meeting down at his offices in the City, I tried again:

Speaking Up gives disabled people a voice so they can make the choices you probably take for granted. Many go on to transform their own lives. We want to triple the number of people with whom we work. To do this we need half a million pounds of your help.

Happily, this second meeting went a lot better than the first and, following long negotiations, I secured significant funding from this particular person. In doing so, I also found I had written our mission statement for the next five years …

To help you to get this right if your Branson moment ever comes, have a go at answering the following questions about your mission:

- How are you helping people?
- What is unique about your venture compared to others working in your field?
- What is important about what you are doing?
- What is the potential of your venture in terms of its scale and impact on people's lives?

Now, imagine the moment of truth is here. You're in a lift with the man himself. You have 30 seconds to get his attention – 'Sir Richard, I have a great idea …' Don't blow it!

Try to keep your elevator pitch to less than 50 words if you can. Finally, have a go at writing out your mission, as it will appear in a business plan. Now it's your turn – do it!

Business goals

Wherever you see a successful business, someone once made a courageous decision.
                                    Peter Drucker, management writer

Goals make your mission into a reality. Goals flow out of your mission and explain, in a bit more detail, what form your mission will take once it is accomplished. A goal is a statement that clearly describes actions to be taken or tasks to be accomplished.

Business goal characteristics are:

- **Derived from the mission statement** – The starting point is to ask 'What do we need in order to accomplish our mission?'
- **Task-oriented** – A business goal must state what is to be accomplished as clearly as possible. Proper goals use action-oriented verbs such as 'deliver', 'implement' and 'produce' rather than fuzzy 'process' terms such as 'facilitate' or 'consider'.
- **Short term** – Goals should be achieved inside three years. Most business plans will have a mixture of time frames for accomplishing goals.
- **Specific** – The better defined a goal is, the easier it will be to understand what is required and to measure success.
- **Challenging** – A goal should challenge the people who are pursuing it. A goal should require considerable effort, but be achievable.

In 2003 I was challenged by a potential investor to come up with five goals that linked back to our vision and strategy. This is how it all looked:

Speaking Up vision

'Speaking Up is working towards a society in which all disabled people have a voice and can control their own lives.'

Speaking Up mission

'Speaking Up's mission from 2004–7 is to achieve a dramatic step change in the numbers of people with whom we work, the locations in which we work and the capacity and sustainability of the organisation.'

Speaking Up goals 2004–7

'1. To become the UK's leading organisation in the disability empowerment sector by the end of 2007 in terms of lives touched and difference made.

2. To develop the organisation's capacity internally into one that scores optimally on an independent measure by the end of 2007.

3. To achieve a national presence, profile and impact comparable with a number of named national charities by the end of 2007.

4. To develop advocacy and consultancy services as major 'social business' areas that secure two-thirds of the charity's income by the end of 2007.

5. To be successful innovators at local level and successful distributors of this learning at national level by the end of 2007.'

Now, remembering your mission, try writing down your goals.

However, identifying goals isn't enough. Each goal also needs to be accompanied by success indicators. These are 'marks in the sand' to prove you've achieved your goals. Below each goal and success indicator you need an action plan stating, broadly, how you'll get there. Here's what one of mine looked like:

Goal 1	To become the UK's leading organisation in the disability empowerment sector by 2008 in terms of lives touched and difference made.
Success indicators (this is what will prove it)	■ To be working directly with 3,000 people per year by 2008. ■ To have services in 20 UK locations by 2008. ■ To understand the impact on every individual with whom we have worked by 2008. ■ To win all major sector awards for our strategy, innovation and quality by 2008. ■ For 90% of our users to rate our services as 'very good' or 'excellent' by 2008.
Action plan (how you're going to do it)	■ To set up five new services each year to 2008. ■ To set up new regional centres in Northern and Central England by 2006. ■ To have introduced a process of impact recording and reporting by 2008. ■ To recruit a sales team to expand services into new locations. ■ To re-brand the organisation and improve its marketing by 2005.

Your year-one plan

Formula for success: under-promise and over-deliver.
Tom Peters, *American management guru*

A good business plan won't include a detailed operating plan for each of the three years ahead. However, it will include a plan for year one. This will enable you to map out the year ahead. It also shows investors that you can do detail as well as big-picture thinking. Most business plans I read are far too optimistic about what can be achieved in the early days.

Here are the first three months of Speaking Up's action plan during our first year:

Month	Key actions
April	■ Establish and equip new office ■ Recruit four new trustees ■ Register as a charity ■ Produce and distribute new marketing leaflet ■ Launch new programme in Fens
May	■ Run PR and event for charity launch ■ Recruit a patron ■ Write a bid to Comic Relief ■ Do research for National Lottery bid
June	■ Submit Lottery bid ■ Run successful launch ■ Run first trustees' meeting ■ Complete first quarter accounts ■ Set up policies for organisation ■ Evaluate Fenland programme

Now set out your main action points for your first year.

Finances – your three-year budget

Most social entrepreneurs hate finances and budgets. We dislike numbers and prefer ideas. But the good thing about finance is that it's not really about numbers. It's about planning your resources. You don't need to be mathematical to be good at this. Even as somebody who very nearly failed GCSE Maths, I grew to enjoy the financial side of Speaking Up. So if I can learn to like it, I am sure you can too!

> *But the good thing about finance is that it's not really about numbers. It's about planning your resources.*

Your business plan will need a three-year budget. In short, the budget explains your outgoings and your income for each of the three years. A budget running that far into the future is, of course, a crystal-ball exercise. However, you should still do it as best you can. Coming up with credible figures will inspire confidence in your reader.

Remember:

■ **Be conservative about income** – The ventures I have seen go down the tubes have always started life with very high predictions of income and slightly depressed expectations of expenditure. The result is that from day one there was a mounting sense of panic as it became clear that the business was never going to 'make budget'.

■ **Include everything** – I have seen many budgets for start-ups that exclude key items and that leave nothing spare for contingency. This can kill your business, so make sure you don't miss a single outgoing.

- **Take care on salary calculations** – It is easy to forget that pay for employees normally goes up each year. Build a 5% uplift into all salaries to be sure. Also, always remember to include 12% employer contributions for national insurance (NI) on all salaries. You would be surprised to see how many budgets I see that forget to include NI and annual uplifts.
- **Create a marketing budget** – This is for all the publicity you will need to attract attention to your new venture. If you forget to account for this, it ends up being taken from other areas.

Here are some budget headings that you can use for your first budget. I'll be covering the finances, including some useful tips on good suppliers and what you should be paying, in Chapter 10.

Expenditure	*Y1*	*Y2*	*Y3*
Staff Salaries National insurance payments (12%) Pension payments (optional) Mileage and staff expenses Volunteer expenses Public liability insurance			
Buildings and equipment Rent (including deposit) Buildings and contents insurance Audit Service charges on building (cleaning etc.) PCs and laptops Mobile phones, office phones and fax Volunteer expenses Venue hire IT support Furniture and fittings Stationery			
Marketing Launch event Design and printing Website Business cards Other Audit Contingency			
Total expenditure			

Income	Y1	Y2	Y3
Grants Contracts Sales/fees Donations Fundraising events			
Total income			

The executive summary

Once you have written your business plan in full, you then have to create an 'executive summary'. This should be the last thing you write, which is why I've put it at the end.

The executive summary is a synopsis of the key points of the entire business plan. The executive summary is not an outline of the plan. Neither is it a cut-and-paste exercise. The end result should be written 'fresh', without large-scale duplication of business-plan content and with a smooth flow of plan highlights from the beginning to the end.

> *The executive summary is a synopsis of the key points of the entire business plan.*

One effective way to begin the executive summary is with an interesting and compelling statement that grabs the reader's attention. This could be an intriguing short story (very short, that is), for example about the life of someone you've helped, including where they were before they came to you. Alternatively, the traditional way to begin the executive summary is with a statement of your purpose, perhaps including your mission statement.

Most business ideas need more than one page to tell the reader what the business is about, but only rarely will more than two pages be required. Make it count – it's your first business plan!

YOUR FIRST BUSINESS PLAN

Could you write a business plan that conveys to the average reader the essence of what you're trying to achieve?

Could you hand it over, confident that people will 'get' what you're doing?

- Your first business plan should give you clarity and confidence. Although it isn't possible to see much beyond a year into the future, the act of writing it will help you identify some of the risks you'll face once you're up and running.
- Your first business plan won't guarantee you success – nothing will. However, just thinking and writing about how you'll create something will improve your chances of making it work.

You can't start a fire without a spark.

Bruce Springsteen, American singer/songwriter

4 **Your founding team**

Wherever smart people work, doors are unlocked.
Steve Wozniak, co-founder of Apple

This chapter looks at the early development of your new venture and the people you need around you during the crucial early years. Mike Southon and Chris West, writers of the bestselling *The Beermat Entrepreneur*,[1] call these special people 'cornerstones'. As on a house, cornerstones make the business anchored and secure. Finding early collaborators who balance you is ideal. But, short of this, you'll need to find ways to work with those you happen to have at your disposal. In this chapter we'll look at the best-known approaches to assessing your own personal style so that you can build a group of early cornerstones who complement you.

Your cornerstones

> *I've been blessed to find people who are smarter than I am, and they help me to execute the vision I have.*
>> *Russell Simmons, American entrepreneur and co-founder of Def Jam*

In a new commercial venture, the four cornerstones would cover finance, sales (or fundraising), innovation and delivery. In a social venture it isn't actually that different. Every social venture, even those dependent on grants, has to sell the idea to someone in order to generate revenue. You will also need people who understand money, operations and innovation.

However, the big difference is that you won't start with four cornerstones. In fact, you'll be lucky to have one. In reality you will be on your own or, at best, working with another couple of people. You may, like me, have to make do with one other cornerstone at the very beginning.

When I started there were two of us working full time, myself and a guy with learning disabilities called James Fletcher. My principles led me to take James on very early but, realistically, Speaking Up wasn't yet ready to support a guy with profound disabilities to work full time. A case of short-term principles coming before long-term survival. Besides James, there was a small number of volunteers.

My early mistake, as well as taking on James too soon, was to try to do all the cornerstone tasks myself, only to fail quite conspicuously in most of them. Despite offers of help, I completed the accounts myself, organised all our operating, attended every sales meeting myself and came up with every single idea. The offers, of course, soon dried up and I ended up pretty exhausted after year one.

---

[1] Mike Southon and Chris West (2005), *The Beermat Entrepreneur*, Prentice Hall.

Not only was I tired but I hadn't made the progress I had hoped for. The accounts were a mess and some of our customers got a bit nervous. Looking back, the quality of some of the work we did was pretty poor. Furthermore, we didn't get registered as a company and charity because I never got around to it. And I was too busy to come up with bright new ideas. It looked, for a while, like year one might be our last.

So far, so exhausting. The burn-out from year one made me think. I took a long holiday in India. While I was gone, I asked a volunteer to do the accounts, which they happily did. I asked another volunteer to lead a couple of our projects, which, again, they did. I came back to find, to my surprise, that I could disappear for a month and things did actually happen. At this point I made a decision to focus on funding and innovation and, by and large, let others do the rest. One year in, I found I had some very effective 'mini-cornerstones'. Within a fairly short time, things had turned around. By the end of the year, I had raised enough money for another permanent member of staff.

The person I chose was 22-year-old Kiwi Stevo O'Rourke, who was, in many respects, my complete opposite. He was my first cornerstone, taking responsibility, in effect, for two of the four key areas, operations and finance, while I focused on sales and innovation. This worked extremely well and we grew quickly. Stevo stayed with me for two years, before returning to his native New Zealand to set up his own business.

It worked because we were so different. Chalk and cheese in fact: I liked football, he liked rugby; he was a Kiwi, I was English; he drank Guinness, I preferred wine. We also had very different strengths, weaknesses and personalities. But in a two-person operation, this was absolutely critical to our future success.

Stevo and Craig – contrasting skills	
STEVO	**CRAIG**
Skills	*Skills*
Good with finances	Good at fundraising
Good with paperwork, processes and setting up new infrastructure	Good at coming up with innovative ideas
Good at planning and delivery	Good at networking and profile-building
Characteristics	*Characteristics*
Calm and methodical	Energetic and chaotic
Reflective, deliberative	Impulsive
Low key	Extrovert
Logical – good at solving problems	Emotional – intuitive response
Able to focus on tasks for a long period	Easily bored by long tasks
Weaknesses	*Weaknesses*
Prone to getting bogged down in a task	Not always in full command of facts
Not always open to opportunity	Runs at opportunities without thinking

Make a similar list of your own skills, characteristics and weaknesses.

Views from the social entrepreneurs

What is your one 'golden nugget' of business advice for people during their first year?

■ **'You need to retain strength, energy, happiness and drive to develop the relationships you need … you also need a roof over your head and a holiday from time to time.'** (Heather Wilkinson, Striding Out)

■ **'Get enough money to survive the early years without having to distort your business model – but not so much money that you don't then go all out for income generation.'** (Martin Clark, Citylife)

■ **'Set yourself a clear and unambiguous vision. Our vision has not changed in 15 years (unlike our bl**dy strapline!)'.** (Julie Stokes, Winston's Wish)

■ **'Make sure you can give total commitment and manage as a business with social outcomes, not a 'Do Good' organisation.'** (Phil Knibb, Alt Valley Community Trust)

■ **'Get the finances spot on, own them, understand them – for they are your friends. Liquidity rather than liquidation!'** (Doug Cresswell, Pure Innovations)

■ **'For the first 11 months, never say no to an opportunity. Then start learning fast what to take on and what not to.'** (Tim West, *Social Enterprise Magazine*)

■ **'Build a strong platform, you cannot move upwards off a blancmange.'** (Steve Ralf, Focus to Work)

■ **'Do anything to survive.'** (Stephen Sears, ECT Group)

What is your type?

If you haven't thought of yourself as a 'type' before, I am inviting you to do so now. You probably conform fairly closely to one of a number of personality types. There are a range of personality tests out there, but the best known is Myers-Briggs Type Index (MBTI). All these tests are done using questionnaires and there are plenty of tests available online. The better ones give you a lot of detail about your particular type. For a bells-and-whistles test, you have to pay, but there are also some good free sites, which give you a basic idea of your personality type. The best of these is to be found on www.businessballs.com. The tests essentially place you on a continuum within the categories shown on the following page, giving you a score for each area.

Define your personality type			
(E)	**Extroversion (E) or introversion (I)?**	■ Do you focus on outside world (E) or inner self (I)? ■ Do you find people energising (E) or somewhat draining (I)?	**(I)**
(S)	**Sensing (S) or intuition (N)?** The way you inform yourself – how you prefer to form a view and receive information.	■ Do you go on observed facts and specifics (S) or what you imagine things can mean (N)?	**(N)**
(T)	**Thinking (T) or feeling (F)?** Your way of deciding – how you prefer to make decisions.	■ Are you objective and tough-minded (T) or friendly and sensitive to others? (F)?	**(F)**
(J)	**Judging (J) or perceiving (P)?** Your method for handling the outside world and particularly for making decisions.	■ Do you evaluate and decide quite soon (J) or continue gathering data and keep options open (P)?	**(P)**

If you do a test, you'll find out which combination of letters you are. It is useful because it can help you to understand yourself better and then recruit people who complement your approach.

Developing your growing team

> *I am easily satisfied with the very best.*
> *Winston Churchill, British Prime Minister 1939–45 and 1951–5*

As you grow beyond your first two employees, you'll need to put together a team that has a single person leading each of the four cornerstone areas: finance, sales (including fundraising), innovation and delivery. You may describe these areas differently, but you'll need, as early as you can, to get a specialist into each of these roles.

Finding such people may be hard. As a new venture, you may find it difficult to attract quality people. Most people still look for secure jobs and a nice working environment and who can blame them? You can't provide this. But, as a new venture, you do have one advantage – and that is the dream you're working to fulfil.

So how do you attract these special people? I managed to attract some great people into the early Speaking Up because I convinced them it was going to grow and make a difference. Lots of people out there are tired of working for large organisations where individuals don't seem to matter. These individuals are your target market. People who ask for a parking space are probably not for you!

Building a balanced team

As well as seeking a variety of skills, you're also trying to find a blend of personalities that work well together. Research by Belbin[2] shows that successful teams are characterised by people who play a variety of different roles.

Role name	Strengths and styles
Coordinator (CO)	Able to get others working to a shared aim; confident, mature
Shaper (SH)	Motivated, energetic, achievement-driven, assertive, competitive
Plant (PL)	Innovative, inventive, creative, original, imaginative, unorthodox, problem solver
Monitor-evaluator (ME)	Serious, prudent, critical thinker, analytical
Implementer (IMP)	Systematic, common sense, loyal, structured, reliable, dependable, practicable, efficient
Resource investigator (RI)	Quick, good communicator, networker, outgoing, affable, seeks and finds options, negotiator
Team worker (TW)	Supportive, sociable, flexible, adaptable, perceptive, listener, calming influence, mediator
Completer-finisher (CF)	Attention to detail, accurate, high standards, quality orientated, delivers to schedule and specification
Specialist (SP)	Technical expert, highly focused capability and knowledge, driven by professional standards and dedication to personal subject area

The simplest central point relating to motivation is that different people respond to different stimuli. Therefore the more we understand about ourselves and other people, the more we understand about what motivates us. People are more motivated and happy when they are performing and working in a way that is natural to them.

---

[2] R. Meredith Belbin (1993), *Team Roles at Work*, Butterworth-Heinemann. www.belbin.com.

Learning to let go

Leaders need to be optimists. Their vision is beyond the present.
Rudy Giuliani, Mayor of New York, September 11 2001

As a social entrepreneur you have a unique relationship to your organisation. The venture is your creation, it feels very personal. You will, at some stage, have done every single job yourself. Relinquishing this can be painful but to succeed, you have to do it. The social entrepreneurs who fail are those without the insight to delegate. Delegation is a price of being a founder, which is one reason why so many founders choose to leave once the venture gets properly on its feet. Leadership by then becomes a different art.

Three periods of leadership

The question 'What makes a good leader?' is asked in classrooms around the world thousands of times a day. The truth, I believe, depends on what is required of that leader. Different situations require different types of leadership. Leaders who succeed in one type of setting flounder in others.

> *For social entrepreneurs, leadership is deeply challenging because our organisations change very rapidly. They can go from one-man bands to big brands in just a few years.*

For social entrepreneurs, leadership is deeply challenging because our organisations change very rapidly. They can go from one-man bands to big brands in just a few years. As leaders of organisations, we have a choice. Either we grow with our organisations or we sign off when we get past our sell-by date as leaders.

My own personal choice was to try to grow with my organisation. I needed to pick up the skills and attributes required for each successive phase. I have characterised this leadership journey as having three key periods:

1. Foundation leadership

The first period I call 'foundation leadership'. During the dreaming and acting stages in an organisation's life, your leadership is primarily about drive, energy and persistence. You're in the trenches getting very dirty. The key resources at this time are your vision and passion for what you're doing. It's definitely not about reflection and listening to other people! George Bernard Shaw summed it up well: 'The reasonable man adapts himself to the world. The unreasonable man persists in trying to adapt the world to himself. Therefore, all progress depends on the unreasonable man.'

2. Builder leadership

This type of leadership is required as you develop the organisation into a sustainable entity. This period relies less on your drive and bloody-mindedness and more on your ability to assemble a well-balanced team around yourself. As a builder-leader it is important that you can listen, reflect and encourage others. Holding onto the gung-ho attitude of the early years may, in fact, endanger your whole venture. The builder-leader is a more rounded, less fanatical figure.

3. Executive leadership

This is the type of leadership required during the replication and growth period. Here you are heading up something much bigger. You have a big role in setting culture but you're doing so through your managers, not your own day-to-day presence. As your organisation grows you are increasingly working as a broker, a chairperson, a maker of compromises between competing interests. You are now a figurehead; a long way from the front-line leader you were in the early days, holed up in your bunker on a do-or-die mission.

Should you stay or go when your venture gets beyond its first three years? A lot depends on whether you personally can make the leap from social entrepreneur to CEO.

Despite finding the shift difficult, I decided to stay on at Speaking Up and to transform myself into a more general manager. When I did my MBA, I found myself a mentor and developed strengths I didn't have before, for instance in operations management. On top of this, I asked for the support of the people in my team, as I do to this day. But, unless you consciously upgrade your skills, it will not be easy for you stay with your venture beyond its early years.

Try the little fun-quiz below that I've devised to test whether you need to stay or go after three years. Tick yes or no to the following statements:

Should I stay or should I go?		
Statement	**Yes**	**No**
I feel constantly frustrated that I can't get anything done anymore	☐	☐
I feel held back by my colleagues	☐	☐
Management bores me but I have to do it	☐	☐
I haven't felt quite right for some time in the role	☐	☐
I find myself always getting involved in development – but it's not my job anymore!	☐	☐
I feel like I have to play referee all the time and I hate it	☐	☐
I just can't understand a lot of what's going on now and I'm not sure if I'm that interested any more	☐	☐
I don't feel like I'm a force for good around here any more	☐	☐
My energy has dropped in the last year or so	☐	☐

If you answer 'yes' to more than three of these statements, it could be time to go. The social entrepreneurs I spoke to were very aware of these questions. They seemed to have an inbuilt certainty about recognising the right time to move on. Jonathan Senker of Advocacy Partners defines that moment as 'When we are talking as much about keeping the project going as the difference it is making'. For Tom Savage, of Bright Green Talent, the time would be 'When the idea comes to you that you could leave and it fills you with relief. The energy's got to be there'. For many, like Rob Harris, of Advocacy Experience 'Sometimes it is just blatantly obvious that it is time to go'.

Clearly, for you, self-awareness and absolute honesty is the key. You need to recruit people who are strong where you are weak. Ideally, the people around you will see the things you don't see so that, together, you can keep the venture on track.

YOUR FOUNDING TEAM

Can you see how your first few appointments will have a huge effect on the success of your venture?

Have you worked out that, if you get these appointments right, you have a massive chance of achieving your vision?

- Get your founding team wrong and it could be all over within three years.
- Whether you have two, three or four cornerstones, they should be people who complement you and to whom you learn to delegate.
- Your founding team will hopefully lead you to a level of maturity where you realise that it's not about you any more, it's about 'us'.

You can't do it all yourself. Don't be afraid to rely on others to accomplish your goals.
Oprah Winfrey, American talk show host and philanthropist

5 Doing good business

Give the public everything you can give them,
keep the place as clean as you can keep it,
keep it friendly.
Walt Disney, creator of Disneyworld

Social enterprises often over-do the social side and forget the business. I've seen it happen before – with disastrous results. By the time you've looked after your needier-than-average staff, there's little left for the paying customer. Result? You lose your customer, swiftly followed by all your staff.

What do successful businesses do?

> *Plans are only good intentions unless they immediately degenerate*
> *into hard work.*
>
> Peter Drucker, management writer

Good businesses, whether they are social or not, do five things extremely well:
1. They obsess about customers' needs and strive hard to make customers very happy. Staff are an integral part of this and, if you are a social business operating without 'free money' in the form of grants, you should only take on as many staff who need a lot of support as you can afford to.
2. They shape their message or brand to fit their target market. Again, the customer is the focus, not the internal people.
3. They achieve the right 'marketing mix' – a blend of price and presentation that outshines the competition.
4. They negotiate good deals. They do not do anything on unfavourable terms. 'Loss-leader' is not in their vocabulary.
5. They deliver their products and services to an exemplary standard.

Note, the focus here is on the business. In social business, the business has to deliver for the social stuff to happen. Never lose track of this.

This chapter looks at each of these five areas and invites you to think about your own venture – however it is constituted – as a business.

> *In social business, the business has to deliver for the social stuff to happen. Never lose track of this.*

Knowing your customer

I think it's very important that whatever you're trying to make or sell or teach has to be basically good. A bad product and you know what? You won't be here in ten years.

Martha Stewart, American businesswoman

As a charity or social business, you probably have at least two types of customer: the people who buy your stuff and the people your business exists to help. Chances are you will have a third type of customer too: people who pay for the 'helping' side of what you do. Typically this will be a donor or a funding body.

All these customers can cause you a dilemma. You can feel, quite frankly, pulled all over the place. The people who buy your stuff, quite rightly, expect an A1 service. Those you help (they, too, are your customers) also present a legitimate demand on your time and energy, particularly if they are employees. And funders will be concerned, above all else, that you are delivering paid-for social outcomes.

This 'triple whammy' of conflicting pressures is a daily reality for most social entrepreneurs. It's a question of how you deal with it. Getting it wrong is quite easy. Focusing exclusively on your paying customers, for example, can upset your beneficiaries and funders. However, an exclusively social focus will, in a fairly short time, kill your business stone dead. You just can't run a successful business without investing proper energy into the commercial side.

This triple whammy is both the defining feature and possible Achilles heel of social enterprise. How social entrepreneurs deal with this is the key to their eventual success.

So how do you do it? Two things stand out. First, it is about keeping the business in balance. Too many social enterprises, like Aspire East of which I was a director, start out with over-ambitious goals on the 'social' side of the equation – in our case supporting lots of homeless people into work. We took a load of people on then found, fairly quickly, that we could not fulfil the business side of the equation – satisfying paying customers who expected a decent service – while having so many high-maintenance people on our books. The end result was an out-of-kilter business that eventually lost its customers and, not long after that, the jobs of all the homeless people. Looking back, I am convinced that Aspire East could have succeeded in providing secure jobs for homeless people had it focused on the business side early on and persuaded its funders, and certain trustees, to allow it to build up the numbers of homeless employees as and when the business could handle them.

Second, therefore, it is about being brutally honest about what is achievable and reaching a settlement, both internally and externally, about how to deal with the triple whammy. This means having honest discussions with beneficiaries about what is achievable on the social side in the early days of a business. It means persuading funders that they need to pay the full costs of the work you are doing with beneficiaries – including costs incurred by focusing on beneficiaries' needs above the needs of the business. Alternatively, funders should see their money as a strategic grant, not funding for short-term outcomes. It means reminding trustees that although they may be motivated by social goals, they have to be patient and give priority, in the short term, to creating a strong business.

There is only one non-negotiable element in all of these discussions – that you, as a social entrepreneur, will do whatever is necessary to survive as a business, even if you achieve nothing socially at first. Because if you don't survive, your chances of ever achieving any kind of social change are nil. However, if you manage, somehow, to keep afloat, even when you are delivering next-to-nothing in social benefit, you keep open the opportunity to achieve massively in the future.

So back to customers – how do you focus on them? Whoever your customer is, the principles are the same. It is about empathy and understanding: stepping into their shoes. One way for social entrepreneurs to understand their customers is to live among them. Many social entrepreneurs, like Phil Knibb of Alt Valley Community Trust in Liverpool, have lived most of their lives in the areas where they now deliver their services. Another is to survey your customers. Interview them. Run a focus group. Get to know their problems.

I learned about our customers – who are disabled people – by immersing myself for a couple of years in the lives of disabled people. I worked as a care assistant. I spoke to disabled activists and academics. I read extensively about the position of disabled people in society. My conclusion was that disabled people didn't really want more resources. Rather, they wanted to have a voice in order to get control over their lives. This was the founding insight of Speaking Up and remains, to this day, the focus of our work with users.

> *My conclusion was that disabled people didn't really want more resources. Rather, they wanted to have a voice in order to get control over their lives.*

When you're trying to understand your funders (for they are also customers) empathy is still important. Most commissioners or grant-givers have an organisational agenda. Their success depends on investing in things that fit with this. Therefore, your job is to work out what these agendas might be. This involves listening very carefully to what commissioners are saying. Often, there is a happy coincidence between their needs and those of your customers. I credit much of the success of Speaking Up to the skill of our people in being able to match the requirements of third-party customers with those of our users.

The challenge comes, of course, when there is some kind of clash between the needs of your users and the requirements of commissioners and funders. The answer normally lies in some form of compromise whereby they can satisfy their agenda while you can do *most* of what you want to do, too.

The key in these situations is not to get too purist. You should demonstrate a real understanding of the funder's issues. Indeed, you get a lot more back that

> *You'd think that looking after customers would come easily to most organisations. It is, after all, the key to success.*

way. There are occasions, however, when you will not be able to square the circle. It is always better to be honest about this and pull back than to risk alienating either your users or funders.

You'd think that looking after customers would come easily to most organisations. It is, after all, the key to success. But, as your own experiences will tell you, it is a pleasant surprise to receive good service as it happens relatively rarely. For example, when you eat out, how often do you experience both a good meal *and* fantastic service?

I cover the nuts and bolts of how to deliver a good service elsewhere in this book, but it starts with the right culture. Management effort, for me, begins and ends with culture. Without a powerful customer-pleasing culture other agendas can, quite easily, dominate the organisation.

For a short time a few years ago, Speaking Up culture became incredibly inward-focused. A need to improve the organisation internally took priority over everything else. Everybody's eyes went off the ball as we worried about processes, systems and people's job descriptions. Getting these things right was important for the long term. However, we definitely lost ground with customers during that time. The learning here is that if internal stuff fills your mind for too long, you lose track of the customers' needs. And once you do this, you're half-way to losing their business.

On the following page is a useful exercise to help you think about your customers. I did one for Speaking Up. Jot down some thoughts on a piece of paper about your customers.

Thinking about customers			
	Users	*Funders*	*Paying customers*
Who are our customers?	Disabled people who are deprived of choice	Government, trusts	Local authorities, Primary Care Trusts
Why do they come to us?	They like our friendly style of service We put them in control of key decisions	We have a great reputation for innovation We understand the policy agenda	We are great to deal with We have a reputation for quality and value
Where else could they go to get their needs met?	Other disability charities	Other disability charities	Other advocacy providers
What things do our customers worry about? Where's the 'pain'?	Dealing with the system Being patronised and ignored	Failing to meet targets Spending money badly	Being stuck with the wrong provider
How can we remove their 'pain'?	Giving them a voice and supporting them through the system	Helping them to meet targets	Being a safe spend Meeting policy goals
What does this mean for how we run our business?	We deliver exceptional personal service	We cultivate very close relationships with funders	We look after our customers very well

Building a reputation

Reputation, you will find, is everything. That is one reason it is so hard at first. You simply don't have one. But you will have one, very quickly and it is up to you what that will be. I asked some of our panel how they had gone about building their own reputation. For Elizabeth Laskar of Ethical Fashion Foundation is was about being trusted. 'We always kept to our mission and vision. Being your word, being what you say you are and working with integrity is important.' Likewise, Miles Hanson of the Collaboration Company gained his 'by never, ever letting anyone down'. For others, like Doug Cresswell, it is about quality. 'You stand or fall by quality. If people know you really mean to do the right thing and slog hard every day to move closer to a better standard, then they are likely to trust you to take over their services and look after their people.' Likewise, Simon Fenton-Jones of Streetshine points to 'Maintaining as professional a service as possible and allowing my staff to tell their stories'.

The marketing mix

The 'marketing mix' is a useful way to think about what your new venture is offering. Think of your services as having four dimensions:

- **Product** – What are you offering to the customer?
- **Price** – What do you need to charge to supply the service?
- **Place** – Where is the customer going to 'shop' for your product?
- **Promotion** – How are you going to encourage customers to buy your products?

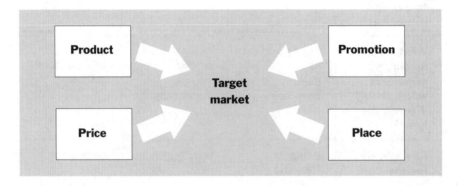

The decisions you make about all the above, when put together, constitute the marketing mix for your products or services. You can choose your own marketing mix. The usefulness of the marketing mix as a framework is that it forces to you get really clear about how you're going to address your target audience. Once you've had a first go at creating a marketing mix, you can more easily see any potential flaws. Your marketing mix will form an essential part of your business plan. Within the mix will lie some of the keys to success for your new venture.

Let's look now at the types of decisions you'll need to make under each of the headings of product, price, place and promotion.

Product/ service	Price	Place	Promotion
What is benefit of your product or service to the customer?	What do you need to charge?	Where are the customers to be found?	Will you sell directly to customers?
What level of quality will you offer?	Will you offer discounts?	Which channels will you use to find them?	Will you promote through advertising and PR?
How will you present your product/service?	Will you increase prices over time?	What motivates the customers?	What kind of budget is needed?

Here is a marketing mix I did for Speaking Up's new advocacy services five years ago:

Product/ service	Price	Place	Promotion
What is the benefit of your service to the customer? We are more professional than other organisations and offer national back-up	**What do you need to charge?** More than small local providers, less than big national charities	**Where are the customers to be found?** Commissioners in local authorities, PCTs and independent sector providers	**Will you sell directly to customers?** Yes, this is the only way to sell this service Tenders play a major role
What level of quality will you offer? Superlative quality, step change in what market currently offers	**Will you offer discounts?** Yes, if you sign up for three to five years	**Which channels will you use to find them?** Mailshots Targeting individuals	**Will you promote through advertising and PR?** Limited advertising Appearance at sector-wide events
How will you present your service? As a professional product in a tired provider market	**Will you increase prices over time?** Only in line with our costs	**What motivates the customers?** Need for a dependable service and empathy	**What kind of budget is needed?** Substantial investment in sales force

Now I suggest you try a marketing mix of your own.

Defining your brand

A brand for a company is like a reputation for a person. You earn reputation by trying to do hard things well.

Jeff Bezos, founder of Amazon

Think of the biggest brands in the world. Now consider what the brand represents. My own favourite brand is Innocent, the smoothie people. Their brand says that they're nice, normal, non-corporate people who want to give people real fruit smoothies. I totally trust them to give my little daughter, Ruby, a lovely, delicious product with no rubbish in it. I like this company so much I am willing to pay a pound more than I would for their rivals' drinks. I have never met a single person from Innocent but, through careful branding, they have managed to convey all this to me. This is the power of branding.

So what relevance does branding have to your new venture? In short, everything. Because, as Jeff Bezos states, your brand is your reputation. It's what you're known for. Brand is not just about having an expensive logo. It goes deeper than that. Brand is about the values and feelings people associate with your charity or business' name. Your brand is communicated in the way your organisation sounds and acts. At the outset of your new venture, you have to make some decisions about your own brand.

Here is a framework to think through some of your branding issues. Again, I have used Speaking Up as an example.

Question	Speaking Up
How do you want to be perceived?	Innovative, entrepreneurial, ambitious, committed to exceptional service
What do you stand for as an organisation?	The belief that people can change their lives if they have a voice
How do you sound and act in front of customers?	Can-do, excited, action-orientated
Does the language, logo and literature you use reinforce your brand?	Yes
Does your internal culture reflect your brand?	Mostly

If you want to do some more detailed self-questionnaires on branding visit www.allaboutbranding.com.

Negotiating good deals

Let us never negotiate out of fear. But let us never fear to negotiate.
John F Kennedy, American President 1960–3

We've all done it at some stage – agreed a bad deal where we end up kicking ourselves that we haven't held out for more. Or, almost as bad, come out the outright 'winner' in a negotiation, leaving the other party feeling they don't want to work with us ever again. My own past is littered with bad deals. I like to please people and, until I learned how to negotiate, I would agree to almost anything to avoid awkwardness. This once resulted in me accepting a nominal fee for Speaking Up to host a new organisation until it was strong enough to compete with us – which it duly did. The whole thing left me sore and resentful. The relationship with the other organisation never recovered, which, in the end, hurt both them and us. Had I got more of what I really wanted, I am sure that relationship would have been going strong today.

So what are the hallmarks of a good deal? One view sees it as simply getting what you want at the expense of the other side. This is sometimes called 'win-lose' or 'zero-sum' because of the assumption that the 'pie' is finite, so one person's gain results in another person's loss.

Another view, set out by Roger Fisher, William Ury and Bill Patton in *Getting to Yes*[1], says that most of the time it is possible and necessary to pursue a 'win-win' approach. This is because it is in the real interests of everybody involved to gain the commitment of all sides to the agreement. Failing to do this risks the agreement breaking down at some later date.

Overall, the message around negotiation is to:

- Know what you hope to achieve from any given deal;
- Know what the other side is looking to achieve;
- Think win-win – find ways to increase the size of the pie so you all get some of what you want;
- Know your BATNA (best alternative to a negotiated agreement) and use this as your benchmark throughout the meeting.

Negotiating contracts

In life you don't get what you deserve, you get what you negotiate.
Chester L Karrass, writer

Nowhere is negotiation more important than in the drawing up of contracts. A contract is a binding legal agreement which normally specifies deliverables, price and timing of payment. It also enshrines the balance of risk carried by each party.

[1] Roger Fisher, William Ury and Bill Patton (2003), *Getting to Yes*, Random House.

Here are some tips to follow when agreeing contracts:

1. Ask for payment in advance rather than in arrears. If you can only be paid in arrears, insist on monthly invoicing.
2. Ask for payment terms of 28 days on invoices with interest recoverable on late payment.
3. Ask for the contract to be viewed as a fixed price for deliverables, not a budget to be clawed over for savings during the life of the contract.
4. Ask for a long multi-year contract (three to five years is ideal).
5. Get a legal adviser to check the contract over if it's for anything over a few thousand pounds.
6. Ask for any one-sided clauses to be omitted or changed so that the risk is shared equally between the partners.
7. Ensure that there is a six month notice period either way inserted into any long-term contract with a stipulation that the party ending the contract meets any associated costs, such as redundancies.
8. Specify the conditions under which the contract might be terminated without the obligations to meet associated costs.
9. Ask for regular review meetings to be inserted as part of the contract.
10. Ensure there is a conflict resolution mechanism inserted into the contract so that it can't be ended until a reasonable process has been gone through with you.

All of these are the hallmarks of a good contract. Of course, you need to ensure that what you're agreeing to do for the price is deliverable. Failure to deliver leaves your charity or social business open to a legal claim for non-compliance.

Names matter

Your brand values will emerge partly from your mission and partly from the decisions that you make about how you want to be perceived. You need to choose a brand image that is consistent with this. A massive decision for you will be the name of your new venture. Names really matter. Every year, organisations spend hundreds of thousands of pounds getting rid of old names and finding new ones.

Here are a few of the better-known ones. Judge for yourself whether they work and are better than the previous ones:

- The Royal Mail – Consignia;
- National Schizophrenic Fellowship – Rethink;
- Mental After Care Association – Together;
- National Council for Civil Liberties – Liberty;
- The Spastics Society – Scope;
- National Children's Home – NCH.

Take time to find the right name for your venture. Try to avoid acronyms. A name needs to be memorable and lively. Here are some good examples of great names of new ventures:

- Kids Company;
- Women Like Us;
- OWL – Opportunities Without Limits;
- Magic Breakfast;
- Pure Innovations;
- Streetshine;
- Heart 'n Soul.

While it isn't obvious just from their names what these organisations actually do, this doesn't matter – because the name, on its own, doesn't have to convey everything. But it does need to stick in the mind.

DOING GOOD BUSINESS

When it comes to doing good business, do certain things stand out very clearly to you?

Isn't it obvious that your customers want dealings with you to be pleasant and easy and that you need to be someone they are always glad to see?

- That old cliché is true; it's all about looking after your customers.
- To do good business your customers need to believe that you'll value them and look after them.
- When doing good business your customers like to be heard and listened to.
- As Bill Gates correctly said, 'Your most unhappy customers are your greatest source of learning'.

I became a vegan and at the same time I realised, gosh, Whole Foods has got to create a higher standard here. I think it will ultimately be a good business decision because I think our customers expect us, want us, to pave this path.

John Mackey, founder of Whole Foods

6 Finding investment or funding

I went to the local development committee and said I had this great idea to build the eighth wonder of the world (in Cornwall). I had no business plan, but said they had to believe me that it was going to be absolutely fantastic. They gave me £25,000 to go away.

Tim Smit, founder of the Eden Project

This is a longer chapter, so bear with me. The future of your fledgling social enterprise may well depend on what you pick up here. And, believe me, when it comes to fundraising, you're going to need every last bit of knowledge and information you can get.

Getting early funding or investment for your venture will probably be one of your biggest early challenges. In this chapter I will guide you through this minefield. While I won't be able to pinpoint exactly where to go or who to talk to, you should, by the end, feel a bit more confident about how to start. Throughout the chapter, I'll include some input from a panel of funders and lenders.

Doing it the hard way – Speaking Up's funding story

Like nearly all new ventures, in the early days Speaking Up ran on passion, not money. We were all volunteers, so the only cash needed was to pay for coffee and bus fares. However, we soon saw that without regular flows of income, even this wouldn't last.

My life as a fundraiser had begun. To learn more, I looked around at local organisations. I saw that a lot of their money came from a handful of recurrent grants from councils and charitable trusts. Digging a little deeper, I also noticed some profound differences between organisations that didn't grow or thrive – I called them the 'strugglers' – and those that did – the 'strivers'.

This is a story of one day, over ten years ago. In the morning I went to see 'Strugglers Ltd'. This organisation was based in a dank, unkempt office covered in scruffy posters from a by-gone era. A surly 'worker' (they always called their people 'workers') told me to wait and did not offer me a cup of tea. After I had waited 20 minutes for the boss to come off the phone, the 'coordinator' (never CEO) of Strugglers Ltd led me into her office. She was an unsmiling type who had, somehow, once managed to impress an interview panel. In our conversation, she was preoccupied in a very morose way with organisational survival. Occasionally, the phone rang and she would answer it. Like all the strugglers I visited, she had a fervent belief that 'The government should pay for this'. Pessimism oozed from every pore. She went on to tell me that the funding situation was so 'desperately dire' that I ought to give up my dream of Speaking Up and go get a job instead. During this meeting, the Strugglers Ltd coordintor did not tell me about her organisation's mission and why it mattered. I recall leaving Strugglers Ltd's tatty little office no wiser about what their organisation actually did than when I had walked in.

In the afternoon, I visited 'Strivers Ltd'. Their offices had a different feel to them. Energy radiated from staff and volunteers. There were smiles, a leaflet to read, a fresh cup of tea while I waited, bright posters on the wall. The organisation was headed by a nice, friendly CEO who could tell me in five seconds what she was up to and why it mattered. She reflected a positive attitude, a sense of possibility. Most crucially, she showed a willingness to help and put me in touch with key people who were helping her organisation. The basic attitude of Strivers Ltd was not one of entitlement. Rather, it was that they *should* be able to sell themselves to people in order to achieve their social mission. Their energy went on developing the profile, image and networks needed to move forward.

Before I had raised a penny, here were the first four lessons in fundraising that I gleaned from the strivers.

1. The importance of networking

Strivers do this naturally, accumulating a powerful group of allies and supporters. I would agree with Carole Stone, author of the *Ultimate Guide to Successful Networking*[1], that it is about mutual aid – making the most out of people you meet to the advantage of everyone. The key skill isn't working out what *you need from others* (that should be easy) but working out what *others might need from you*. Great networkers are generous to others as they hope others might be to them.

I learned that networking is a key skill in fundraising. It's a great source of up-to-date, often fairly exclusive, information. It puts you in touch with potential supporters. A strong personal network will ensure that you have at your disposal the network of each individual within your own.

> *A strong personal network will ensure that you have at your disposal the network of each individual within your own.*

Following my visits, I put this learning to work. I mapped out who might know the people I needed to support Speaking Up. The word of friends seemed to open doors. To my surprise, everyone I asked through my network was willing to take my call. The mention from an associate was really important. By saying 'yes' to me, they were helping their associate. Also, I found that people liked to be asked for their help and advice.

Before long I was meeting fairly senior people and telling them all about the vision I had for Speaking Up. Often, I would be accompanied by somebody we'd helped so that they could tell their own story. Within a very short time, I

[1] Carole Stone (2004), *The UIltimate Guide to Successful Networking*, Vermilion.

had the support of a handful of key people, all of whom had access to funding. Jenny Gupta, at that time a head of the council's learning disability service and later a trustee of Speaking Up, was one of them:

Speaking Up came from nowhere. They were very clear about what they were seeking to do and how I could help. They told me they needed allies in the local authority who could help them to gain a foothold. Of course, they also needed money, with which I could also assist them, on a small scale at first, as I wanted to see if their actions matched their words. And they did!

Supporters like Jenny Gupta kept popping up for us, as they will for you when you're actively networking and promoting what you're doing in urgent, positive terms.

Very soon, we had persuaded the local NHS and a handful of smaller trusts and foundations to back us.

2. The importance of raising your profile

The strivers taught me that being known and understood is a prerequisite to raising money. Profile-raising also enables you to punch well above your weight as an organisation. Having a big profile shows a certain competence in defining your key purposes which, in turn, helps a funder to feel more confident about you.

The good thing about profile-raising is that virtually any organisation of any size can do it, with a little imagination. The challenge for us was to create a clear association with the words 'Speaking Up'. In the end, we devised a media event that got us onto the front page of our local newspaper. This involved a number of disabled people rolling a 100-foot mock shopping receipt down the steps of the town hall. This highlighted the amount of weekly shopping that extra council charges would cost disabled people. It made the TV news and forced a statement from the head of the council. Nobody again said 'Who are Speaking Up?' Interestingly, the council increased their funding to us considerably the following year!

> *What is the key to a good profile-raising event? If you want the media involved, you've got to create a story for them.*

What is the key to a good profile-raising event? If you want the media involved, you've got to create a story for them. Real human stories are the lifeblood of the media. Charities often forget this and try to promote interest in their activities, rather than their stories. Then they wonder why the media don't bite ... Put yourself in a journalist's shoes: what will get her readers interested in your organisation?

3. The importance of being able to sell

The strivers I met were natural salespeople. They combined an easy manner with a clarity and sense of purpose that commanded my attention. Like most things, selling is a skill that can be learned. I have always followed the words of my friend Mike Southon, author of *Sales on a Beermat*.[2] The principles of selling, he says, are very simple:

- **Be liked** – People buy from people they like, never those who they don't. Therefore, make sure you build a pleasurable connection with people from whom you're asking something.
- **Qualify** – Ensure you're talking to the right person. Don't waste time and energy talking to the person who isn't the decision-maker.
- **Close** – Make the ask. We often avoid cutting to the chase, especially if money is involved. But the cliché is true – if you don't ask, you don't get.

The sales meeting

So, you're there, the big meeting. You've got half an hour. What do you actually do? My advice is to spend no more than five minutes explaining your vision and mission. Most people can't take much more than a five-minute speech. Stick to the real basics – who you are, your vision – and use personal stories to show your vision in action. Even highly intellectual people like to hear inspiring stories. Don't rely too much on facts and figures at this stage, just a couple of 'killer stats' (e.g. 'Do you know that 95% of the prison population has mental health problems?'). Don't use PowerPoint presentations. Most people find them tiresome and there's a big risk that something won't work properly.

Towards the end of your short presentation, turn the focus onto your host: how can you help your potential funder? Most people have a number of problems for which they need solutions. It is often clear upon meeting them what these are. Say where you might be able to help. If the problems are not apparent, ask them. Then think quickly about how you could help.

After the presentation, the meeting should evolve into a conversation. At this stage, you'll know if the person might be interested in what you have to offer. Their body language will be positive. There will be no signs of boredom. They'll be sitting up, listening, trying to connect. Now it's time for you to stop and to give them time to ask questions or talk themselves. Listen really carefully to what they say, even if it doesn't seem immediately relevant. Hidden in there may be an opportunity.

One such opportunity came up in an early meeting with a man who ran part of the local NHS. After my presentation, the guy told me his concerns about how people were building new lives in the community following long stays in hospital. It was clear he was genuinely perplexed by this issue. I simply offered to help. 'How?' he asked. Thinking quickly, I suggested that we observe what was happening with this group of people and report back. We had never done this before, but it was just a matter of applying our principles to a new type of activity. The man was impressed and asked me to write a proposal, which he then funded with tens of thousands of pounds. This funding was paid 100% upfront and provided the security needed to rent an office and pay myself a small allowance until I could find some real wages. The learning

---

[2] Mike Southon and Chris West, *Sales on a Beermat*, Random House, 2005.

point here? It is important to listen and think on your feet about how you can help people.

It's also important to conclude any first meeting with a clear sense of where you are with somebody – is this the beginning of something or just a useful fact-finding mission? If the latter, you need to make it clear what the next step might be. The atmosphere of the meeting may give you a clear indicator one way or the other, but even if it's been really good, you need to ask for something, even if it's just another meeting, or another contact. People expect to be asked and, again, they are more likely to say yes if you ask. But making the ask is difficult for most of us – me included. A lot of us duck it for fear of spoiling the moment. We'd rather float off on a vibe of positivism with no clear answer than risk a cold shower of rejection.

Good 'closures' or concluding phrases are things like: 'I feel our meeting has gone well today and I want, if I can, to see if we could reach some agreement about where we could go next with this. This is just an idea but … do you think you could …?'

Ending on a positive note is always important. Always leave a business card and some printed literature about your organisation.

Views from the funders and investors

What can brand new organisations do to help sell their activities to funders?

- **'Chance your arm! Reach out and network. Get in front of people and convince others of the merits of your work.'** (Mark Ereira-Guyer, ex Lloyds TSB Foundation, now EG Consulting)

- **'Be realistic and look for incremental growth. Show you have done some work already – such as a feasibility study, a pilot, voluntary effort and so on. If you can't be bothered to put the effort in, why should someone else fund it? Tell us about your track record as an individual and that of others involved.'** (Nicola Pollock, Programme Director, Esmée Fairbairn Foundation)

- **'Stress your innovation, your competence, your willingness to learn and change.'** (David Gold, Glimmer of Hope)

- **'Demonstrate the need. Have a fundraising plan. Show you have some relevant experience. Plus you need to be clear why you're not going to do it through existing organisations.'** (John Kingston, Venturesome)

- **'There are a few options here: demonstrate the track record of the people involved; provide references; offer convincing market research, which demonstrates the need for the services; and turn it into a positive – innovation, energy and freshness are often highly valued by funders,'** (Dan Gregory, Futurebuilders)

4. Attitude is everything

The reason the strugglers fail to raise enough funds isn't to do with intellectual ability or unpopular causes. It's a difference in attitude. You don't have to be a genius to raise money (indeed it may not even help!).

You don't have to be a genius to raise money (indeed it may not even help!). However, you do need the right attitude.

However, you do need the right attitude. This starts by accepting, deep-down, the fact that you don't have a right to exist. Nobody owes you or your organisation a bean. Accept this and you're half-way there. Strivers see themselves in a tough market against lots of worthwhile causes. They realise that a case has to be made. From here, the right attitude involves a level of enthusiasm and enjoyment. As you'll see, funders can detect this. It inspires them. They like individuals and organisations that present themselves in a positive and compelling way.

Writing bids to funders or investors

Whether you're a charity or a social business, there's a big chance that you'll need to do a lot of this yourself, particularly early on. The challenge is that in bureaucratic organisations, like the Big Lottery Fund, it's often hard to pull on personal relationships. Indeed many funding organisations will often, publicly at least, discourage this.

Without wishing to strike a deterring note, fundraising is becoming more and more competitive in the UK. The number of charities seeking funding has grown from 98,000 in 1991 to 168,000 in 2005. Only 400 charitable trusts in the UK give more than £400,000 per year. Therefore, as a new, small organisation, your odds are long – 67% of all funding and public donations go to the top 2%, the big-brand charities. Applicants to many trusts have as little as a one in ten chance of success.

Faced with this, what do you do? How should you approach the myriad of funding agencies out there? How should you prioritise? How do you differentiate yourself? Well, before you start applying anywhere, you need to do a number of things.

Before you write your bid

1. Do a fundraising strategy

Most organisations, even new ones, consist of a number of different work-streams. You need to break your venture down into fundable blocks of work. How you cut it is up to you. But you need to be able to parcel your operations in ways that make sense as individual projects. You can do this geographically, or by client group or by nature of activity. Then you need to plot these against available pots of funding so that you can package up what you're doing in a way that maximises the fundraising opportunities available.

2. Develop a budget that includes all your costs

It is quite common, especially early on, to just ask for the costs of a project without asking for full organisational overheads. People sometimes don't know how much to pitch these as or think they'll do better if these are excluded. Don't make that mistake. I did and it almost bankrupted Speaking Up. These days, most funders are fairly clued up about your need to recover costs. Indeed, they are as likely to penalise you for excluding them as to reward you. You can download the Full Cost Recovery formula from the following website (www.fullcostrecovery.org.uk). This will help you set a proportion of all of your costs against each bid you write.

3. Research possible funding organisations

When faced with a large number of possible sources of funding it is tempting to adopt a 'scattergun' approach. However, it is far better to identify a small number of funders that seem a good fit. The best guides to funding are produced by Directory of Social Change and can be ordered from their website (www.dsc.org.uk). These directories make clear what trusts will and won't fund, what format they like bids to be in, when to apply and, often, the amount of funding on offer. Sometimes, they list people you can speak to before you apply.

A day spent with one of these books identifying potential funders is a great investment of your time. If you have a bit more money, you may wish to invest in some grant-finding software such as trustfunding.org.uk, Funder Finder or Grant-Finder. These systems will search web databases using the criteria you enter. Often, your local council for voluntary services will have these web subscriptions or software for members to access free. The early searches I did for Speaking Up ten years ago helped us to identify several organisations that continue to fund us today, so it's well worthwhile.

4. Research the need

You have become a social entrepreneur for a reason. Know your reason inside out. You need to be able to describe, in exact terms, the nature of the need you're in business to meet. This is your 'market' and you have to be authoritative – if it's a local need, you need to have spoken to local people, done small surveys and so on. If your cause is broader-based you need to have done your homework. This will include knowing what others are doing about the problem (it's unlikely that you'll be the only person in your field). Once you've done this, you must be able to talk about the need in a convincing way. As a new social entrepreneur, you need big statistics, personal examples or stories, an explanation of why others are failing and why it's right that you should set up this enterprise yourself. All this needs to find its way into your bids and presentations. Without this grip on the issues, you'll lose the one thing that sells you to funders the most – your authenticity.

Views from the funders and investors

What would you say to new applicants about what they need to get right before they approach you?

- **'Be clear about what you are aiming to achieve – in terms of the social benefits and the business model. Many bids focus on one aspect – social or business – almost to the exclusion of the other.'** (Nicola Pollock, Programme Director, Esmée Fairbairn Foundation)

- **'Understanding of what we as a funder are trying to achieve and respecting the guidelines.'** (David Gold, Glimmer of Hope)

- **'Clarity of thinking and of nature of the ask. I don't want to have to guess the answer to "Who are you? What's the history? What are you trying to achieve? What's the project? Why do you need the money?" Work these out first.'** (John Kingston, Venturesome)

- **'They need to a) know exactly what they want: from the work to be done to the amount of money required; and b) understand our eligibility criteria and our application process. Then match the two together and see if they fit! Done.'** (Dan Gregory, Futurebuilders)

- **'Research, have ideas and a good sense of what the appropriate responses should be to identified needs or problems they are seeking to address.'** (Mark Ereira-Guyer, ex Lloyds TSB Foundation, now EG Consulting)

When you're writing your bid

1. Follow bid guidelines

This is a bit like saying to people sitting an exam, 'Answer the question'. It seems obvious, but it's surprising how many people fail to do this and render their bid useless. I have, once or twice, done it myself. Not only do you miss out but you have to recover your credibility, too. Nearly all organisations that give or lend money invest a lot of time in their guidance to applicants. To ignore this goes down rather badly. So whatever you do, stick to the brief rigidly.

2. Assume they know nothing about you

When you're setting up your organisation you live and breathe it. This is fine until you start trying to talk to other people who find you deeply obscure. Every funder I know says they have to pore over most applications several times before they 'get it', by which time they are not best disposed towards the applicant.

> *Remember that you're writing for a person.*

Remember that you're writing for a person. This person is, at best, an intelligent onlooker, not a specialist. They need the basics spelled out to them. This includes who you are and what you do, an overview of your sector and a clear sense of where you fit into it. If they 'get it' first time, you're ahead on points already.

3. Think 'inputs, outputs and outcomes'

It is easy to write bids that don't differentiate between the above. This results in a confusing jumble. Funders increasingly look at potential projects, both formally and informally, under these headings. So make it easier and spell it out for them. One of the most frequent confusions is between outputs and outcomes. Think of outputs as your services or products; think of outcomes as what happens as a result of that service or product.

Project	Inputs	Outputs	Outcomes
Mentoring for work project for serial offenders (one-year programme)	1 full-time coordinator Organisational overheads 10 volunteer expenses Meeting room x 50 hires Specialist trainers for volunteers Publicity and marketing materials	10 serial offenders to receive 26 mentoring sessions Each offender to produce a life-plan during mentoring Each volunteer to receive 6 weeks of intensive training Each offender to be accompanied to visit 3 workplaces 9 people complete the course	8 report increased self-confidence 7 attend job interviews during the period 6 find employment 5 are still in employment after six months 5 of the trained mentors are used on a future course

If you can think like this, you'll be able to build the clarity you need to convince funders that your project is worth backing. Some funders, such as the Big Lottery Fund, ask explicitly that you do this, but it is worth doing it for any bid as it will increase your chances of success.

4. Find a good name for your project

Right from the beginning at Speaking Up we have always racked our brains for good project names. It's odd, but these do matter more than you might think. Get it right and your project will appear energetic and imaginative. For example, a local charity near us called their new computer recycling project 'Reboot'. A less imaginative charity would, I am sure, have called it something dreadful like CRASP – the Computer Recycling and Sale Project. There's a lot in a name, as any successful business will tell you. Whatever you do, avoid that scourge of the voluntary sector, the acronym.

> *Whatever you do, avoid that scourge of the voluntary sector, the acronym.*

5. Write in a compelling style

This means imposing a few rules on yourself. No long, rambling sentences and strictly one idea per sentence. No fancy language or terminology that you need a degree to understand. You need to see your written work as a meeting with your reader. It has to be something that is simple to read and inspires confidence. It if doesn't, then you will come across as a third-rate communicator. Imagine that your writing is yourself in person. You either hold someone's attention or you don't. You are interesting if you can be understood and if your passion and energy finds its way onto the page. When you've written a bid, give it to somebody you trust and who works in another field to be critical. Never send a first draft that nobody else has read. Let nothing leave the door that you don't think is well written. If it isn't a great piece of writing, then expect the bid to be rejected.

> *Imagine that your writing is yourself in person. You either hold someone's attention or you don't.*

Views from the funders and investors

What separates the 20% of best bids from the rest?

- 'A successful bid is readable and jargon free, clear and to the point and not too long. Unsuccessful ones tend to be hard to read, with unsubstantiated generalities and aspirational, rather than grounded and specific. They are often over-optimistic about income projections and unrealistic about marketing and growth.' (Nicola Pollock, Programme Director, Esmée Fairbairn Foundation)

- 'A successful bid will be able to demonstrate, passion, clarity, "feeling the issues" and a clear vision of what success looks like.' (David Gold, Glimmer of Hope)

- 'Clarity of what the work is about. Clarity of direction strategically. Clarity of financial need.' (John Kingston, Venturesome)

- 'The most successful bids are those that most clearly demonstrate that they consistently and undeniably meet the criteria of the fund – they utterly convince us they hit our criteria bang on the nose. After that, it's about a well-constructed and clear, jargon-free business plan, which does not leave questions unanswered. Typically this would include: organisation's history, mission and objectives; risk analysis; evidence of market research and evidence of need; details of key staff and trustees; clear and concise multi-year cash flow forecasts (with explanation of assumptions where necessary); and a clear understanding of costs.' (Dan Gregory, Futurebuilders)

- 'Looking like you mean it! The evident presence of passion, purpose, solutions and sincerity. Having a keen sense of what they can really do to tackle their cause or problem.' (Mark Ereira-Guyer, ex Lloyds TSB Foundation, now EG Consulting)

So, you've written your bid

1. Before you send it, check it

Have you checked it for spelling and grammar? Do the budget and the words all make sense when viewed together? Have you included absolutely everything being asked for? Be really careful at this stage. You've invested a lot of time, so ensure the bid isn't spoilt by a silly error or missing piece of information. Ensure that you present everything professionally. First impressions will count. Send it recorded delivery. Again, this shows care.

2. Call to check it's got there

This is a good idea and a way of possibly getting into conversation to discuss the bid with a funder. A positive interaction at this stage is important because it means you are likely to be remembered more than the others who haven't called. Be careful though. If the person at the other end of the phone doesn't want to talk or seems keen to get away, respect this and keep it brief.

3. Make the most of the interview

This doesn't always happen but is fairly common. It's also your big opportunity to impress. This sometimes takes place on the telephone. If you're offered this, then ask if they would conduct the interview in person. Grants officers secretly love getting out of the office! If they insist on the dreaded telephone interview, make sure they brief you on the questions first, so you can have everything you need to hand. This matters. It's easy to get flustered on the telephone as you search for budgets or job descriptions. On a phone line this sounds really awful and often labels you as disorganised. If they come to see you in person, this is your big chance. The impression they form on the visit will shape their decision. Of this, have no doubt. Therefore, make sure they meet some of the people you're helping. Take them to where something interesting is going on that day. If need be, arrange it especially for them. Do a plan for the visit and send it in advance, along with really clear instructions of how to find you and a travel plan for where they are coming from. Collect them from the nearest station. If they are driving, cone off a parking space near to your office. Remember, if things go wrong for them en-route they will arrive in a negative frame of mind. It's your job to make sure they get to you without any problems.

The impression they form on the visit will shape their decision. Of this, have no doubt.

Once they have arrived, make sure the offices are tidy and you have a room free from interruption. During a visit from Comic Relief, I remember a 32-person Brazilian Samba band striking up next door to where I had booked the meeting. The walls shook. Fortunately, we decamped to a café and all was well. So do check everything out. During the meeting, have all papers to hand, two copies, one for them, one for you. Don't waste precious time having to go to fetch things.

The interview is the very best opportunity you'll get to sell your project. Therefore, treat it like a sales meeting. Be liked. Most funders would deny that there is a personal element to their decision-making but all my experience suggests the opposite. Empathise. Put yourself, for a second, in the funders' shoes. They have extremely limited resources. While willing to take risks, most funders seek to minimise exposure. They do this by rigorous analysis of the information put forward. Therefore, answer all their questions directly and honestly, even if you know you're not as strong in some areas as you'd like to be. If you're in any way embellishing, this may be sensed and will work against you. In my experience, funders look for integrity and a sense of reality in the people they eventually support. If they believe in your fundamental honesty and sensibility, they are far more likely to back you than if they're not sure. Credibility is everything.

> *The interview is the very best opportunity you'll get to sell your project.*

4. Start creating the relationship

You've done it! They gave you the money. This can be a one-night stand, or the start of a beautiful relationship. Which way it goes is down to you. See the grant period as being like a courtship. It gives you the opportunity to get to know each other and, if it goes well, take the next step towards a long-term commitment. On the whole, funders are not by nature promiscuous or flighty. They prefer long-term relationships, particularly if the first few dates have gone well. While they will seldom make the running, they appreciate your constant attention. If you're struggling to find the time, reflect on how much work it would take to replace this funder if you lost them. If you're trusted, they are keen to hear your proposals for the next stage, when they are ready. The best funders closely identify with your vision and, after three years, often want to make you family. These principles apply to any funder, investor or business customer – be they trusts and foundations, individual donors, corporates or government. Funders are among your most important customers. Treat them like customers and they'll come back for more.

> *The best funders closely identify with your vision and, after three years, often want to make you family.*

By following these rules at Speaking Up we grew our grant and contract income from nothing to £3 million in ten years, with most of this added during the last three years. We enjoy long-term relationships with a large number of organisations. A major reason for this is that we do really interesting and life-changing work. But that alone is not enough. As well as being good at changing lives, you've also got to be even better to deal with – nicer, easier, more enjoyable than everyone else. This costs you nothing, so why not do it?

Where to go to find funding

Whether you're running a new charity or a business seeking investment, you will probably need to find the right organisations to help you. So where can you go?

Grant-making trusts

As I mentioned, there are a number of guides and web-based products – these list about 400 trusts that give most of the UK's grants. Besides these, there are small amounts available for specific causes and geographies but not a lot for the average organisation.

Trusts vary widely in their character. Some are distinctly old fashioned in their approach to grant giving. Their trustees read like a page of *Who's Who* and there's a whiff of old money to them. Phone calls to these trusts are often answered by very posh people who are, in most cases, extremely nice. With one or two exceptions, however, I have tended to find these trusts hard to break into. They tend to give idiosyncratically, often in line with the personal interests of their trustees. You can spot this by looking at their published list of interests. If you see 'disabled children' and 'the rare spotted Norfolk vole' on the same list, then the trust is best avoided... (unless you are setting up in one of these areas!). Some of these trusts discourage unsolicited applications altogether. Unless you've got a contact, you may struggle.

> *If you see 'disabled children' and 'the rare spotted Norfolk vole' on the same list, then the trust is best avoided...*

However, old money trusts are less and less the norm. Many are now increasingly professional. The grant sector has been transformed in the last fifteen years by big new players such as the Big Lottery Fund and Comic Relief. These organisations have led the way in publishing strategic priorities and holding these for three to five years. Processes of application are clear, transparent and open. If you are not of blue blood, these more modern and transparent trusts are your best bet, particularly when starting out.

The Big Lottery Fund is by far the biggest, giving £630 million a year. I can safely say that Speaking Up would never have got to where it is without the Lottery. Two early strategic grants got us from start-up through the early phases. The Big Lottery Fund has transformed the landscape for social entrepreneurs and is still a good place to look for money if your organisation is in its early days. One in four bids to its Reaching Communities fund is successful.

> *The Big Lottery Fund has transformed the landscape for social entrepreneurs and is still a good place to look for money if your organisation is in its early days. One in four bids to its Reaching Communities fund is successful.*

I am deliberately not going to talk more here about all the different charitable trusts because there are too many to list. My advice, though, is to single out a small number of trusts relevant to your area and go for it. Always include trusts specific to your geography even if they don't specify what they give to. Being local is normally enough. In any given area there are usually a small number of trusts dedicated to local causes. Lists of these should come up in any decent search.

Funds aimed at start-ups

These are limited in number and in the amounts they can make available, but a handful of organisations is now specialising in helping social entrepreneurs. The most eminent of these by far is UnLtd, which provide two types of grant: initial sums of up to £5,000 for start-ups; and then 'level 2' grants of up to £20,000 once the start-up period is over.

UnLtd

UnLtd – the foundation for social entrepreneurs – wants to support and develop the role of social entrepreneurs as a force for positive change in the United Kingdom. It does this by providing:

- awards to social entrepreneurs;
- a UK-wide fellowship of people who have received awards;
- research into the impact of social entrepreneurs on society;
- UnLtd ventures.

UnLtd was set up with a £100-million endowment from the government several years ago. The money offered comes with a package of support and mentoring.

Their level 1 awards are aimed at individuals or informal groups of people who have an idea that will change society for the better, and want help in getting it off the ground. The awards can be used for the things you need to start or develop your project: materials, equipment, renting rooms for meetings and so on.

Level 2 awards support individuals whose ideas are already off the ground and who now want help to take them to the next level. A level 2 award can pay for the living expenses of award winners to help them devote more time to their projects.

A level 3 award is up to £60,000. This also brings with it a package of mentoring and business guidance. For more information see www.unltd.org.uk.

Other trusts that explicitly support start-ups include the Novas Scarman Group (www.novas.org) and the Glimmer of Hope trust (London only) (www.aglimmerofhope.org).

Venture philanthropy organisations

Venture philanthropy is a cousin of venture capitalism and has recently been successfully imported into the UK by the Impetus Trust (www.impetus.org.uk). Speaking Up benefited from support from the

Impetus Trust after we'd been in existence for five years. Most venture philanthropy organisations specialise in existing rather than new organisations. Other venture philanthropy organisations include New Philanthropy Capital (www.philanthropycapital.org), the Private Equity Foundation, Ark (Absolute Return for Kids), Institute of Philanthropy and Breakthrough! (www.can-online.org.uk). They all specialise in strategic grant making, not loans.

Venture philanthropists work by putting both money and business expertise into an organisation. They work on the premise that it is possible, with the right investment and management, to create high yields of 'social value' in relation to the initial investment. To give an example, Impetus put £400,000 into Speaking Up over four years, during which we increased our turnover from £500,000 to £3 million. Impetus Trust's investment and expertise catalysed this growth.

Government and Europe
You can apply to a large number of local, national and European government funds. An increasing number of these deal not only in grants but also loans and, most recently, 'quasi equity', where you only pay back if you're successful.

Central government
Government funding, like government itself, is notoriously complicated. To make it easier, there is a Directory of Social Change website, currently government-funded, called www.governmentfunding.org.uk to help you navigate through the myriad schemes out there. Many of these schemes are run by government departments such as the Social Enterprise Pathfinder, operated by the Department of Health (www.dh.gov.uk/en/Managingyourorganisation/Commissioning/Socialenterprise). They have no problem about you getting in touch first, which you should do. Due to the Compact and the Office of the Third Sector, the government seems to be more in touch with the sector than ever before, so there's no danger of a Sir Humphrey Appleby type on the phone these days. The good thing about dealing with central government departments is that they normally issue fairly clear guidelines. The bad thing is that they will rarely come to see you and don't engage easily once you've got the grant, making them difficult to turn into repeat funders.

'Arms-length' agencies
Funds for third sector organisations are being increasingly run through 'arms-length' agencies (or quangos) such as regional development agencies, (www.englandsrdas.com), Futurebuilders (www.futurebuilders-england.org.uk) and Adventure Capital Fund (www.adventurecapitalfund.org.uk). Proving increasingly useful to social entrepreneurs, these are explicitly set up to assist organisations seeking new solutions to old problems. All have missions that commit them to helping organisations become sustainable and take their ideas to scale. As a new venture, you should look closely at all these sources.

Local government

Once upon a time, local government was a rich source of grant aid for small organisations. Two such local authority grants helped Speaking Up to get through our difficult first three years. Sadly for some, those days are fast coming to a close. Grants are being replaced by contracts and service level agreements, which define the social benefits to be exchanged for the council's cash. While this has put paid to a minority of organisations that did very little, it has also made it harder to get money for new ventures that have no track record.

> *The good news is that where grants were once a bit of a closed shop, the new contract culture enables you to make your case.*

The good news is that, where grants were once a bit of a closed shop, the new contract culture enables you to make your case. If you're a new venture with energy, purpose and skills, you can probably out-perform existing local organisations with relative ease. If, like me, you have no problems about putting paid to organisations that are past their sell-by date, then you may even enjoy winning your first service level agreement.

European funding

European funding was once a mainstay for many new organisations, particularly those operating in deprived parts of the UK. While this will continue until 2014, the overall amount is falling considerably as the new accession countries of Eastern Europe come on board.

The thing to remember with European funding is that it requires a surprising amount of time to manage. The paperwork is extensive and often difficult to administer. The final downside is that you often get the cash many months after applying. Plus, if the people in Brussels aren't happy with your returns (and they are often not) you might never get paid at all.

While European funding has no doubt helped transform many run-down parts of the UK, I've seen many organisations nearly go bust due to problems with late and non-payment. As a start-up, approach European funding with some caution. If you do go down this route, think about cushioning your risk by acting in a partnership where you are, in effect, a subcontractor of another UK organisation.

> *My advice is that, unless you personally know somebody very well placed, you should put your early energy into other forms of fundraising.*

Corporates

For a start-up, a relationship with a big company is difficult to achieve without a contact at the very top. Above all, corporates value your brand and the benefits of its association with them. If you're new – and, of course, unknown – you're not a lot of use to them. Because of this corporates won't be able to do very much for you, beyond perhaps an initial donation.

My advice is that, unless you personally know

somebody very well placed, you should put your early energy into other forms of fundraising. Later on, once you are better known and easier for them to understand, they may be able to see a connection between your brand and theirs. Until that time, it will be hard for you to persuade them to put a lot of money your way.

If you do choose to pursue corporate backing at an early stage, there are three rules to stick by:

1. Recognise that it will probably be slow work because there are no deadlines and you will be the one driving it.
2. Look for win-win. Even the most responsible corporates like their giving to tie in with their own objectives, be it employee volunteering or promoting their own brand.
3. The investment they give normally needs to have a PR payback. For corporations to sign cheques for anything more than trivial amounts, they need lots of opportunities to attach their company publicly to the work you're doing.

High-net-worth individuals

High-net-worth individuals are different again. The number-one challenge for all is access to these well-protected people. There is now a record number of millionaires in the UK but they give at relatively low levels compared to those in the USA. Your biggest chance of finding one is through a personal contact. Should you be lucky enough to do so, it is then a question of whether or not they are interested in what you're doing. You should be able to find out whether they will meet you through your contact. If they will you've got a significant chance of getting support. Then it's back to sales skills.

If you're successful, it is important to agree the benefactor's role. If you want them to give the money as a donation, not invest it as an owner or even a co-owner, make this very clear. As a donor, they don't control the organisation, or you, for that matter.

Loans

Loans are a relatively new area of opportunity for social entrepreneurs. Traditionally, Speaking Up mainly had to rely on grants or contracts. High street banks wouldn't touch us unless the loan was secured against the assets of the organisation. Today, the social enterprise finance sector is coming to life with a range of newly available instruments.

Loans are increasingly available from a wide range of sources. Some are similar to high street loans and carry a similar rate of interest, the difference being a more understanding and patient approach.

However, more interestingly, increasing numbers of lenders are now willing to take a higher risk. Once such lender is Venturesome (www.cafonline.org), which lends to individuals and businesses they believe have potential. The good thing about this type of lender is the long-term nature of their involvement, the flexible terms of repayment, and the fact that if it all goes

> *As a social entrepreneur, you have to make a big decision about whether loans are right at the early stage of your business.*

wrong they won't take away your home!

Notwithstanding this, any lender is going to be very wary about giving away money if they think it unlikely they will get it back. As a social entrepreneur, you have to make a big decision about whether loans are right at the early stage of your business.

There's a good chance that loans might be right, as they are with many businesses that need loans for basic capital items and a small amount of money with which to operate the business day to day. Social entrepreneurs who can achieve strong early sales and a strong surplus of income over expenditure in the first three years may well suit loan financing.

Conversely, those whose new ventures are unlikely to achieve surpluses, or whose activities are inherently in need of long-term subsidy, should be more cautious with loans, particularly when grants would, in practice, work better. This applies to a good many social entrepreneurs who, like me, are dealing with the extremities of market failure, where it is not always possible to solve social problems in a way that enables surpluses to be generated easily.

Quasi equity

Quasi equity is useful for social entrepreneurs who are working in areas where there is a high potential for growth but also a significant risk that the venture will not become financially viable.

Quasi equity works like this: The investor gives you a sum of money to implement your business plan. If things go well, you return the whole of the money plus, possibly, a high level of interest as a reward for the investor's risk. Conversely, if things go badly, the lender will lose the sum of money lent and have no right to pursue your organisation for defaulting on the loan.

> *If you're not confident about one day repaying your quasi equity investor, it may be better, at this stage, to seek a non-repayable grant.*

Is quasi equity for you? It may be. It is preferable to a loan but only if you are genuinely doubtful about being able to pay the money back. If you're confident about repayment, you may as well take a loan at a low rate of interest. If you're not confident about one day repaying your quasi equity investor, it may be better, at this stage, to seek a non-repayable grant.

Quasi equity providers work across a range of the sectors listed above: grant making, government and venture philanthropy.

We're all doing it

In the end, how do you get funders interested in your organisation? As social entrepreneurs, nearly all of us have to do this.

Best to hear it from the horse's mouth: 'By talking about real people and being honest about what we can do', says Jonathan Senker of Advocacy

Partners. For Doug Cresswell, of Pure Innovations, it's 'hard bidding – write great tenders, stun people at interview and then live up to the expectations you have set in people's minds, because that's when the job really starts'. Luljeta Nuzi, of Shpresa, believes that you have to 'be yourself, let passion speak for you, read what they fund, be able to sell your project in no more than three minutes. Use different methods to make them feel what you feel'.

FINDING INVESTMENT OR FUNDING

As you've read this, have you been thinking about how best to secure the funding you need for the first few years?

Do you think you could identify some potential funders and put together a strategy for your fundraising?

- Finding funding is all about writing a strong bid and delivering a compelling presentation.
- Finding funding is never easy but it does get easier; especially when the words of current funders are ringing in your ears.

Everyone lives by selling something.

Robert Louis Stephenson, author

7 Deciding on a legal structure

If you build that foundation, both the moral and the ethical foundation, as well as the business foundation, and the experience foundation, then the building won't crumble.

Henry Kravis, founder of KKR (Kohlberg Kravis Roberts and Co)

It's not something I boast about but it took me four years to register Speaking Up as a legal entity. For two of those years our income was tiny, so it didn't matter. But for the other two I was running quite a decent-sized organisation as a personal concern.

Like many people setting out, I was bamboozled by the whole business of registering the organisation. Everyone I spoke to seemed to say something different. Amid the frantic activity of those early years, getting registered just slipped onto the 'too difficult' pile. Eventually, I listed us as a charity and a company limited by guarantee, a structure we've stuck with to this day.

Today, there's a lot of advice about legal structure for social entrepreneurs, including an excellent 70-page booklet by the Social Enterprise Coalition called 'Keeping it legal'[1] (www.socialenterprise.org.uk). This takes you through the options in extensive detail. I thoroughly recommend that you read it.

Here though, I'll take you quickly through the main issues you need to consider now if you're not registered. If you already are, it will be a good test of whether you've got the right structure for your activities.

The difference between incorporated and unincorporated structures

As the founder of a new venture you will need to decide upon the most suitable structure within which to place it. If you start as an unincorporated association, you need to know that you will be carrying all the responsibilities of the organisation personally.

Incorporation, the act of putting your new venture into a company, puts clear legal water between you and your venture. As such, your new venture can, in its own right, enter contracts or agreements with others. The business can, in its own right, sue and be sued, employ people and make them redundant, accumulate surpluses or make losses.

Here are some reasons why you may *not* want to incorporate:

1. **Income is tiny** – Your turnover may be so low, particularly early on, that you are not putting your personal finances on the line. This was the case for me and it made sense during the earliest time of Speaking Up not to incorporate.

---

[1] 'Keeping it legal – a guide to legal forms for social enterprises' (2006), Social Enterprise Coalition.

2. **Tax advantages** – As an unincorporated sole trader you can pay tax in arrears. You also pay lower personal national insurance contributions and may offset any losses against tax paid in previous years.
3. **Low regulation** – You don't need to file annual returns and accounts by law to Companies House if you remain unincorporated.

If you stay unincorporated, these are the forms your venture can take.

- **Sole trader** – You can trade under the name of your venture, but the business is under your personal ownership and control.
- **Partnership** – This is the same as above, except it involves more than one of you. There is often an agreement between partners. If there isn't, something called the Partnership Act comes into play. There are no registration requirements.
- **Unincorporated associations** – These are groups that come together for a shared purpose. They normally have a constitution and an elected board, or a management committee. Collectively, the management committee is liable, as individuals, for the venture. A lot of social enterprises and charities start in this form.

What are the benefits of incorporation?

The Social Enterprise Coalition lists six of these:

1. **Legal personality** – Your venture can be a legal entity in its own right, entering its own agreements, employing staff and so on.
2. **Limitation of risk** – If you incorporate, you can contain the risks associated with your venture. You're no longer at financial risk personally if things go wrong.
3. **Clarity around mission and governance** – If you incorporate, you're able to put a statement of how your venture is to be run into a legal document. This prevents anyone changing this informally at a later date.
4. **Developing a sense of ownership** – Incorporation means you are free to define who can, in effect, be owners of the venture.
5. **Public accountability** – If you incorporate, you have to publish information about yourself. This may help the public to view you as worthy of trust and support, as a social purpose organisation.
6. **Recognition by financial institutions and investors** – If you're trying to raise loans or other types of investment, you may need to incorporate so that lenders have a clear sense of who they are dealing with.

Three years in at Speaking Up, the benefits of incorporation were clear. It made total sense for the risks associated with employing increasing numbers of staff to be tied into a new legal entity. We also wanted to protect the mission and governance arrangements from future tampering. Furthermore, incorporation enabled us to extend formal ownership and control beyond the handful of people who set it up. Finally, we needed both the public and our funders to feel confident they were dealing with an organisation that was accountable and demonstrably run in the public interest.

So, if you do choose to incorporate, what are your options? Broadly speaking, there are two main options: the company and, less commonly, the industrial and provident society (the IPS).

Before I go on, I want to explain why becoming a registered charity is not on this particular list. Becoming a charity is not a form of incorporation. It is a status in law given to certain types of *activities*. You do not have to be incorporated to be a charity. Equally you can be incorporated and not be a charity. Charitable status is about what you *do*, not what you *are*, in terms of organisational type. When people say 'We're a charity', they in fact mean that their activities have charitable status according to the list of 13 charitable purposes in the Charities Bill of 2006. I'll come to talk about charitable status later in the chapter.

> *Becoming a charity is not a form of incorporation. It is a status in law given to certain types of activities.*

The company

There are three principal options if you want to incorporate your venture as a company: company limited by shares (CLS); company limited by guarantee (CLG); and either of these forms can also be incorporated as a community interest company (CIC).

The company limited by shares

In a CLS you and your co-founders own the company's 'share capital'. This is often set nominally at £100 upon foundation but can grow depending on a future valuation of the company and its assets. This makes you and your co-founders private shareholders. The nature of the split (50:50, 60:40, 25% each etc.) is decided at this stage.

Most private businesses and large public limited companies (plcs) are CLSs. The purpose of the CLS is to enable you to own your own business. It is your property. As such, you can buy or sell your share of the company reflecting its value in the marketplace. For you, it opens the possibility of making money from a future sale of your share in the company.

The good news for you as an owner or shareholder in a CLS is that the maximum you can lose is your investment. If a company collapses with a mountain of debts, liability to pay these off doesn't extend to you personally, except in very unusual circumstances.

A small number of social entrepreneurs go down this route. Several of those interviewed for this book have done so, including Tom Savage of Bright Green Talent and Miles Hanson of the Collaboration Company. This, of course, gives them the option to extract profit for their personal use, as well as investing in social purposes.

For this reason, the law doesn't currently see such private entrepreneurs as proper social entrepreneurs, regardless of how much good they choose to do either with their profits or their company's time. I, however, prefer to look at their social achievements not their legal structure when making my judgement.

The company limited by guarantee

In a CLG there are no privately owned shares in the sense just outlined. The value of the share capital stays the same – normally £1 – even if the company becomes big and successful. Therefore, members of the company who own the 'shares' (generally the management committee) cannot personally profit from the increased value of the company. And, like any shareholder, their liability for any losses is limited to their stake in the company.

The CLG has long been associated with the voluntary and community sectors. The appeal of the CLG format is that it frees you to find members of your board who are motivated by your social mission but will only join you if they are protected from personal liability if things go wrong.

In a CLG you, as founder, are allowed to be a member of the company yourself. Under this arrangement your ownership and control is shared equally in law with every other member. However, this means, in effect, that your own personal investment up to the point of incorporation (the blood, the sweat, the tears) won't be reflected in the amount of formal power you have in the company. At best, you're just one of several equal members. Not exactly a rich reward if you've been the founding force of a new CLG! This is in sharp contrast to the situation for a private entrepreneur setting up a CLS. This person would probably own all or most of the shares and have total control of the business. In a CLG, on the other hand, you can kiss goodbye to the possibility of either total control or long-term financial recognition as founder, like I did.

But if you're seeking a situation where you're in full control or where you wish to sell at a later date, the CLG is not the right structure for you.

For most social entrepreneurs, this won't be a problem. But if you're seeking a situation where you're in full control or where you wish to sell at a later date, the CLG is not the right structure for you.

YOU'RE NO LONGER IN CONTROL I'M AFRAID...

The community interest company

The CIC is a relatively new format aimed specifically at social entrepreneurs who want to remain in full control of their organisations. One thousand of these were registered by July 2007. Scores of new ones are being registered each month.

The CIC has a number of distinctive features. First, it must serve the community interest and report in detail on this to a special CIC regulator. Second, the CIC can be either a CLS or a CLG.

However, if the CIC is a CLS, there are major limitations on how much you personally can benefit from your own allocation of shares. Firstly, there is a 'lock' on assets. This means that any annual dividends are no more than 35% of overall profits. The remaining 65% is retained in the company and used for community purposes.

Furthermore, your shares in a CIC cannot be sold at a significant profit, even if the company has been successful under your stewardship. So, even if you put in money at a point where everything looked very risky, you cannot be rewarded with the real market value of your company when you sell it, even if your shares in the business are now worth millions of pounds. All you'll get instead is your money back plus no more than 4% above the Bank of England base rate for every year you have left money in the company. In a CIC, the relationship between risk and return is more or less eliminated.

Third, like a normal company, a CIC is empowered to accept large injections of equity finance in exchange for an agreed stake in the company. However, unlike a normal company, there are legal limits on the growth in value of any long-term equity investment, as explained just now.

Is the CIC right for you? That will depend on a number of things. If it is important for you to retain ownership and control of your venture while also receiving a salary, it could be right for you.

Likewise, if your venture isn't explicitly charitable but has streams of work that benefit the community, it could be right for you. The CIC label would enable you to be very clear about the public benefit side of your business. It will open up funding opportunities that would be closed to you as a private business.

> *The CIC label would enable you to be very clear about the public benefit side of your business. It will open up funding opportunities which would be closed to you as a private business.*

Finally, it will depend on your investment needs. If you need a large amount of start-up investment or early working capital, you may need to attract equity funding where you trade investment for a stake in the business. As a simple CLG, you cannot do this (the share capital is fixed at £1 per share), but as a CIC limited by shares you can. And, as a social entrepreneur, the beauty of a CIC is that your investors can only take modest returns. Therefore, if you use their investment to create massive added value, you leave the bulk of gains made through an investment on the balance sheet of the company to be used for future reinvestment or social benefit.

The industrial and provident society

An IPS is a completely different type of legal entity. It is a 'society' not a company. It takes one of two forms: a community benefit society or a cooperative society. The difference is that the first is set up to benefit the whole community while the second is for the benefit of its members.

To set up as an IPS, you need to have a special reason for not registering as a company. Above all, this is normally the desire to operate on the cooperative lines of one member, one vote, regardless of contribution or ownership.

As in a CLS, it is possible for members of cooperatives to own up to £20,000 of share capital. As with a CLG, members of community benefit societies hold only nominal share capital.

Why might you consider setting up as an IPS? As an organisation, you may have an ethos that lends itself to the democratic and participative ideals associated with this organisational form. You may also feel that, while it is important to have a certain level of share capital yourself, it is important that you are equal in your voting rights with other members. In other corporate forms, such as the CLS, it is not possible both to own high levels of share capital and be an equal voting member with those who have less.

Other advantages of the IPS are that it is possible to protect the mission more fully by building in a bigger majority for change than you can with a CLS or a CLG. Finally, the fact that you won't need to register as a charity in addition reduces the amount of regulation that you face.

Relatively few social entrepreneurs set themselves up as an IPS, in comparison to CLGs, CLSs and now CICs.

Relatively few social entrepreneurs set themselves up as an IPS, in comparison to CLGs, CLSs and now CICs. The CLG, coupled with charitable status, is still a very popular model and perhaps the better understood, compared to its nearest IPS alternative, the community benefit society. For those social entrepreneurs seeking to cement their own control or to take out value down the line, the CIC with shares is in some ways a better alternative to the IPS. It puts fewer limits on the scope of your ownership and is probably better understood in the public mind than a cooperative.

How about charitable status?

An organisation can be a charity if it has exclusively charitable goals. These are defined in the Charities Act 2006 (see www.charity-commission.gov.uk) and now cover 13 areas. The directors of organisations that become charities are known as trustees. The key feature of charities is that any surplus following payment of all bills or debts must be either held in reserve or re-invested in the purposes of the charity.

In 2006, 64% of social enterprises were also charities. Charitable status is not available to CICs and CLSs. Charities are regulated by the Charities Commission and organisations with an income of more than £250,000 need to provide detailed annual returns each year.

There are big upsides to charitable status if you're a social entrepreneur:
- Your venture is exempt from any tax on surpluses or bank interest;
- Donations attract gift aid;
- You get at least 80% relief from business rates;
- You are eligible for many grants;
- You have a clear 'brand' in the public mind;
- Despite a recent drop in public trust in charities, the overall level of confidence is still high. By becoming a charity you are immediately identifiable by the person in the street as a known 'good cause'.

But there are downsides to charitable status too. If you're a founder who is now employed by the organisation, registering your venture as a charity means you're no longer allowed to be on the board of trustees.

Other downsides of becoming a charity include:
- **Doubling in regulation** – You have to report to *both* Companies House and the Charities Commission every year. Your accounts are also subject to the SORP regulations.
- **Not possible to raise equity** – This is challenging if you need a large equity-type investment in order to grow the organisation that cannot be obtained by grants or donations.
- **Charity brand not always helpful** – Some social enterprises trying to present themselves as businesses can feel that charitable status gives the wrong message to their key audiences.

For more detailed information on this, see the *DSC Guide to Charitable Status* by Julian Blake[2] of Bates, Wells and Braithwaite Solicitors.

So, what is the right legal format for you?

This will depend on a number of things in combination:
- The balance of your mission between social and commercial goals;
- Your own need for control over strategy and decision making;
- The extent to which you care about owning a share in the venture;
- Your need for equity investment;
- Your need for grants and donations;
- The ethos and values of your new venture in terms of participation.

Below are a couple of tools to help you find the legal format that suits you best: a table showing you at a glance the different legal formats, and various scenarios that may describe your situation, with recommendations.

---

[2] Julian Blake (2006), *Charitable Status*, Directory of Social Change.

Comparison of legal forms for social enterprises

	Company limited by share (CLS)	Company limited by guarantee (CLG)	Industrial and provident community benefit society	Industrial and provident cooperative society	Unincorporated association	Community interest company /CLG	Community interest company /CLS
Incorporated with own legal ID?	Yes	Yes	Yes	Yes	No	Yes	Yes
Limited liability for members?	Yes	Yes	Yes	Yes	No	Yes	Yes
Limited liability for directors/ trustees?	Yes	Yes	Yes	Yes	No	Yes	Yes
Constitutional document?	Memorandum and articles of association	Memorandum and articles of association	Rules	Rules	Rules or constitution	Memorandum and articles of association	Memorandum and articles of association
Objects?	Any	Any	Must benefit community	Must follow co-operative ideals	Any	Community interest	Community interest
Charitable status?	Not usually	Can be	Can be	No	Can be	No	No
Regulator?	Companies House	Companies House	FSA	FSA	None	CIC regulator	CIC regulator
Fees for registration?	£20	£20	£100–£1,000	£100–£1,000	n/a	£35	£35
Debt financing available?	Yes	Yes	Yes	Yes	Yes	Yes	Yes
Equity financing?	Yes	No	No	Yes	Yes	Yes	No
Protection of social purpose?	None guaranteed unless charitable	None guaranteed unless charitable	FSA has to approve changes	FSA has to approve changes	None/safeguards in constitution	As CLG	As CLS
Membership voting?	One vote per share	One member one vote	One member one vote	One member one vote	As per the constitution	As CLS	AS CLG

Source: based on pp 20–1 of *Keeping it legal*[1]

Finding the right legal format

Which of these statements is most like you?

a. 'My venture is only partly socially oriented and my activities wouldn't, for the most part, count as charitable. I don't really need grants but to grow I do need investors who will demand strong equity returns. I am socially minded and will dedicate however much I can afford to community causes – but I also want to sell this thing one day and do well out of it.'
Suggested format: company limited by shares

b. 'My venture is highly socially oriented and our activities are charitable under the Charities Act. I am not personally bothered about having a say in ownership or any share capital but I will need a salary. I need to attract socially minded directors who value limited personal liability. I don't think we'll ever need equity investors.'
Suggested format: company limited by guarantee with charitable status

c. 'My venture is socially oriented but I am keen to retain a personal stake in it. I am not sure if our primary activities would count as charitable. I also need investors but I know I won't be able to offer massive returns. We're a choice for socially aware investors only.'
Suggested format: community interest company (CLS)

d. 'I am setting up something to benefit the members and keen to keep a personal share in my venture as it grows but I am also attracted to cooperative principles whereby everybody in the company, whatever their shareholding, has an equal voice. How we do things matters as much as what we do.'
Suggested format: IPS – cooperative society.

One way or another, you'll make your decision. And, yes, it is a question of balancing your social and financial goals. We all do this differently.

Jonathan Senker, of Advocacy Partners, told me his company is entirely about social goals. 'But without the finance, we won't achieve them. So failing to attend to our financial stability means a dereliction of our social goals also.' Hannah Eyres, of Keyfund, believes that self-sustainability should be a goal for all social entrepreneurs. 'I have seen too many organisations adopt a victim status with regards to funding availability, when really they need to stop moaning about it and take action.' Miles Hanson, of Collaboration Company, reckons that the balance is achieved 'by accepting that doing well and doing good can be two sides of the same coin'.

It all depends upon how you set out your legal stall in the very beginning.

So you've decided what do to, what next?

Registering as a company

This is really straightforward. The two legal documents you need to draw up to set up a new company are called the memorandum of association and the articles of association.

These are standard-type documents, which you just adapt to the specific purposes of your new venture. Together these form your 'constitution'. Within them is detailed your purpose as a company, how you run the company and the circumstances under which the purpose of the company can be changed. It is wise to have these checked by a lawyer before you submit them, to make sure they're spot on. It costs just £20 to incorporate your new venture and same-day incorporation costs £50. You can do it all online for even less at www.companieshouse.gov.uk.

When you set up your company you have to appoint directors, of which you'll be one (if you don't then register as a charity). These are appointed by the shareholders or members. The job of directors is to act in the interests of the company and to exercise 'reasonable care' in their management functions. Every company has to designate one of the directors as chair of the board and have a company secretary who is responsible for the basics of company law compliance, such as filing returns and accounts to HM Customs and Revenue. The secretary needn't be a director. It is usual for the board to delegate management to a managing director, who is often the senior employee below board level.

Regulation as a company is, again, quite easy. You have to file an annual return within 42 days of an annual general meeting, present audited accounts within 10 months of the end of the financial year and notify Companies House of any changes of directors, and changes in your memorandum and articles of association.

Registering as a charity

You go about this by applying to the Charities Commission. Full details are on their website. To be sure of qualifying, you need to ensure that your goals come within the Charities Act 2006. It is not necessary to be a particular type of company to obtain charitable status, but if you're a company limited by shares it is unlikely that you'll qualify, as you won't pass the public interest test in the way you use your assets. As applications to become a charity normally take longer than it takes to register a company, it may be best to do what Speaking Up did and incorporate first then apply for charitable status after that.

Registering as a community interest company

A CIC is registered with Companies House in the same way as an ordinary company. However, you do need to fill in an extra form, which includes a statement that you're pursuing the community's interest, with details of how you're doing it. Companies House then passes the application to the CIC regulator who will decide whether or not you've passed the 'community interest test'. If it decides in your favour, your registration will go through Companies House. If you've already registered as a CLS or a CLG, it is possible to add CIC status. You just need to amend your memorandum and articles of association and submit all the appropriate paperwork to Companies House. After that you'll be regulated by the CIC regulator – this is a 'light touch' regime compared, say, to the Charities Commission, where reporting is more extensive. However, you will need to submit a community interest report each year detailing the pay of your directors, any dividends and interest payments made. You must also explain how you have pursued community interest and involved stakeholders.

Registering as an industrial and provident society

An IPS needs to be registered with the Financial Services Authority (FSA) (www.fsa.gov.uk). Only societies that meet the social criteria set out in the Co-operative and Community Benefit Act 2003 can be registered, and the FSA monitors compliance fairly closely. The FSA retains the power to suspend or cancel your registration if you do not comply. The annual disclosures to be made include an annual financial return within seven months of the end of the financial year plus an auditors report for organisations above £350,000 turnover a year (or £250,000 if they have charitable status).

DECIDING ON A LEGAL STRUCTURE

Any the wiser about the right kind of legal structure for your new venture?

Is it the case that no single structure or format will work perfectly for you?

- It's about choosing the legal structure that, on balance, is most advantageous to your organisation in the long term.
- Ten years after registering Speaking Up, our CLG and charitable status structure still broadly works, though we are open to changing it if we need to.
- Think ahead and think of future flexibility before you make your final choice. Where will you and your venture be in a decade's time?

The winner is the chef who takes the same ingredients as everyone else and produces the best results.

Edward de Bono, philosopher

8 Finding and keeping the best people

Great people + great organisations
= great outcomes
Curt Coffman, American author

You will either know this instinctively or, like me, you may take a few years to wise-up. But if you're going to deliver your vision, you will be doing so largely through the good work of other people.

Not only are people your greatest asset, they are also your most expensive, at up to 80% of your income. This will turn out either to be a great investment, or a disappointing one that leaves the world unchanged. How that investment performs depends on you. If you're anything like I was when I started, you'll probably need to spend more time on your people than you think.

What not to do – the early days of Speaking Up

> *Talented people are attracted to Google because we empower them to change the world.*
>
> *Sergey Brin, Co-founder, Google*

If I had my time again, I would spend a lot more of it getting the basics right. I was one of those founders who had a blasé attitude to people issues. Supervision, training, performance review and appraisal all bored me rigid. It revived memories of the sleepy organisational world from which I had escaped. Plus, I remember saying to myself, 'I never needed any of that stuff to motivate me, why should anyone else?'

This is, of course, pretty naïve. Non-entrepreneurs need a firm structure within which to work. They require a clear job description, regular support and feedback about how they are doing. They also need to feel trusted and empowered to make the big calls where their own work is concerned.

They also need to feel trusted and empowered to make the big calls where their own work is concerned.

My wake up call came five years in when I nearly lost several of our key staff. In our first few years we grew from two employees to about twenty. While a highly informal approach worked well early on, it didn't after we grew beyond 10 people. It took me two years to do anything about this. During this time I tried to run a growing business without any real 'human resources' structures or processes in place. At the end of this, we were in a total mess.

- **Poor working environment** – Our office was probably one of the worst working environments I have ever seen in terms of IT (always down), comfort (either hot or freezing) and overcrowding (we couldn't all physically get into the office at the same time).

- **Bad appointments** – We were living with the consequences of some really poor appointments, due to rushed and sloppy recruitment practices such as not following up references properly. We wanted tigers but ended up with turkeys!
- **Employment tribunals** – We had a damaging employment tribunal to deal with, which was our own fault because we hadn't done things correctly when we needed to let somebody go.
- **Quality problems** – Morale got really low because we weren't supporting people well enough or monitoring what was being achieved. The quality of our work went down. Funders were calling me for 'a quiet word'.
- **People feeling disempowered** – I had, without realising it, turned Speaking Up into a benign dictatorship in which everything led back to me. People didn't feel they could make big decisions about their own work or take initiatives without first putting it to me.

Overall, by neglecting the people side of the business, I put the mission of the organisation at risk. So what did I do to sort it out?

The following five years saw a big turnaround in the way we approached the 'human resources cycle'.

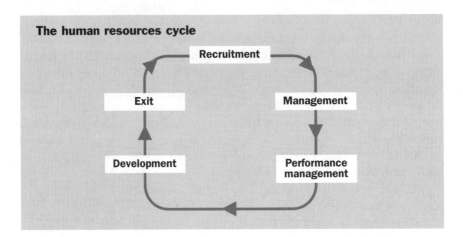

The human resources cycle

- Recruitment
- Management
- Performance management
- Development
- Exit

Recruitment

Focus on selling your values and your vision, and on hiring people whose values are in line with yours; you can teach skills – you can't teach values; hire raw talent – and then invest in that talent.

Hamish Davidson, CEO, Rockpools Ltd

If you're serious about changing the world, finding the right people to do it alongside you is mission-critical. Find the wrong ones and your dream is over.

How do you find them? According to Miles Hanson of the Collaboration Company, it's 'by talking to friends and colleagues about people who they believe would love this kind of work'. For Hannah Eyres, of Keyfund, it's about 'looking in the less obvious places'. Phil Knibb of Alt Valley Community Trust believes in 'growing our own: people can join the organisation to work or learn and generally move through the "ranks" as they gain experience'.

> *If you're serious about changing the world, finding the right people to do it alongside you is mission-critical. Find the wrong ones and your dream is over.*

I am surprised at how laid-back we can be in the third sector about recruitment. We forget that it is a seller's market out there. There are far more jobs than great people to fill them. Yet, in the interview room, charities and social firms sometimes think they hold all the cards. Wrong! This is not *The Apprentice*! You can offer a dream but not a lot more. There will always be easier, better-paid jobs elsewhere. To get the best people, you need to sell the dream.

However busy you are, do make the time to get personally involved in recruitment, especially when you're still quite small (up to 25 people). Too many social entrepreneurs are too happy to leave recruitment to others. Don't. Only you can sell your vision to people. Those first 20 employees will make or break you. So get involved. And be choosy. Like with marriage, if you recruit in haste you will repent at leisure! UK employment law puts a lot of onus on employers when it comes to sorting out any really bad underperformers that slip through the net. This means that if you don't carefully performance-manage these 'turkeys' either to raise their game or get out of the organisation, you may end up, like I have done, in an employment tribunal. So, the recruitment stage is critical.

UNDER – PERFORMANCE BEGINS 12pm

Writing the job spec

Rarely do I get excited by charity or social business job specs. They are often so dry and bureaucratic that they send me to sleep. Few set out a vision. Many list every single aspect of what somebody might possibly do without answering the really important question, namely 'What difference could I make if I took this job?'

The purpose of a job spec is to maximise interest in the job – nothing more. The best job specs encourage the right people to get in touch with you. In earlier times, we at Speaking Up used a template from a local authority that featured categories such as 'limitations of authority' and 'principal accountabilities'. This made our exciting new jobs sound like vacancies in the Albanian state bureaucracy.

We've now ditched this and gone for something a lot simpler and enticing: it should be snappy, fresh and personal. It should be accompanied by a short opening from you, the founder or CEO, saying what an exciting post this is at such a crucial time for the organisation.

Experience not essential!

Write this in bold. Outsiders to the sector are often discouraged by the required level of experience asked for by third sector organisations. Given that nearly 60% of the workforce is in the private sector, you need to think carefully about what is really essential. Do you really need candidates to have three years of third sector experience?

Do you really need candidates to have three years of third sector experience?

Being less specific on experience has enabled us at Speaking Up to recruit across sectors and among younger people. Five out of seven on my management team come from the private sector and about as many of our recruits in 2006 had left education only within the last few years.

Of course, you have to outline the role. As Doug Cresswell of Pure Innovations says, 'You have to be crystal clear on what the job is'. He also believes that 'many of the right people are under your nose just waiting to rise to the next challenge with a little coaching and support'. Reckoning that new blood is getting hard to find, Doug told me he's 'considering poaching successful people like everybody else does!'

Think attitude, not experience

Emphasise the personal qualities and attitude you're looking for as much as knowledge or skills. The latter can be learned, while it is much harder to change people's character or attitude.

Karen Mattison of Women Like Us was keen to point out that 'the kind of people who apply to us for work really care about what we do, and usually relate to the work for personal reasons'.

At Speaking Up we recruit people directly in line with our five core organisational values and spell out the behaviours we expect in people who come to work here.

1. **We are passionate about our mission** – As leaders we act to generate enthusiasm for our mission and communicate its importance both internally and externally.
2. **We want to learn and develop** – As leaders we create a supportive environment where people can voice ideas and opinions, develop and grow.
3. **We are focused on quality** – As leaders we demand and demonstrate high standards and motivate ourselves and our teams to ensure Speaking Up delivers.
4. **We are innovative in solving problems** – As leaders we engage with problems and work positively with other members of Speaking Up to find solutions.
5. **We are taking action to change lives** – As leaders we put the needs of our service users first by communicating openly and honestly and not losing sight of our mission.

Application forms

Again, be careful here. I instinctively prefer to avoid application forms as they put people off getting in touch. Remember that, at this stage, you're seeking interest in the job not a person's life story. So, make the getting in touch as painless as possible. Who wants to spend Sunday afternoon filling in a long-winded form just to get a meeting with you? How would you feel if the tables were turned? A good CV and short covering letter will tell you if you want to meet someone or not.

Advertising the job in the press or online

I worry when I see the way many third sector organisations do this. You see tiny, densely typed ads for obscure-sounding jobs. The sad thing is that these are often great jobs, just badly sold ones. We went from wordy, boring ads to short, sharp snappy ones that made the job sound attractive and fun.

Do invite candidates to get in touch with you. A really interested candidate will often want to give you a call to find out more. Give such people time as they are normally the better candidates.

Advertising isn't cheap, so make sure it works for you.

- Invest in design for the template (normally cheaper than you'd imagine).
- Make your advert eye-catching and fun – remember not to give chapter and verse about the job.
- Negotiate hard. We push advertisers extremely hard to get the best possible deal for us.
- Use free advertising. *The Times Public* runs a free page for charities. *The Guardian* lets you advertise free for volunteers.
- E-mail your ad to all your contacts and ask them to pass it on to anyone they think might be interested.
- Use online advertising – it's cheaper and many people now search for jobs on the Internet.

Assessment and final selection

Shortlisting

Ideally you'll have a pile of at least five to ten decent applications to choose from. Less than this and you're either not paying enough or your job marketing isn't up to scratch. Don't be so rule-bound as to turn away a late applicant. One of our most valued staff was a late applicant. She went on to completely change the direction of our organisation.

When you're shortlisting, keep in mind that you're panning for gold. Unless you are deliberately employing people who are disadvantaged, you need to be looking only for exceptional people. Always meet a high achiever, even if it's in a completely different field. Every high achiever has repeated that success with us. This includes former computer-sales people, parent-carers, teachers, nurses and shop-keepers. Conversely, those we have released have been people with relevant experience but for whom low achievement has been a lifelong pattern.

Perils of the single job interview

One commentator compared the job interview to the used-car salesroom where the blemishes are covered up and confident patter used to skirt round any difficult issues. Sound familiar? All the research into job interviews shows a number of things:

- We tend to select people who are 'like us';
- A single interview doesn't predict how well somebody will do in a job;
- Impressions of people's suitability for a job tend to be gained in the first few seconds of meeting, not on what is said in the interview.

In short, this isn't a process that can be relied upon. All sorts of subconscious prejudices get in the way. This creates enormous risks. At Speaking Up, after a couple of terrible appointments, we abandoned the single interview format.

Instead, we wanted to make recruitment less of a used car-buying experience and more like buying a house, where you at least do a survey first. To this end, we replaced our single interview with a new system.

The two-stage selection process

Invite each of your short-listed people to an initial interview. Go quickly through their application and find out more about what people have *achieved* in the past. Remember, this is the biggest single predictor of future achievement. Also, figure out whether or not you could see that person fitting into a fairly small, new organisation.

Then bring that number down to the four highest achievers and run a simple assessment day, which all the candidates attend together. Any organisation, big or small, should be able to do this – it's just about being organised. The day should have several elements. Each is intended to test candidates in particular skills. The table on the following page shows this.

Assessment day elements	What it tells you
Briefing about your vision and values and why you created the job	See who looks most interested, who asks questions
A 30-minute written test on how they would action a particular issue	How quickly they think and how well they can write
Role play: a presentation back to a meeting on the problem	How they operate in meetings, how deeply they grasp the issues
Lunch with staff and volunteers	How they relate to people generally
Pre-prepared presentation	How they deliver to an audience
Final interview panel	How they cope with close questioning

You then need to rank candidates on their performance at *all* key parts of the day. Invite volunteers and beneficiaries to your panel and, if possible, an external person to provide another perspective.

By the end of the day you should know if you have a winner. This doesn't mean somebody who just ticks all the boxes on the job description. It is also someone who shares the vision and values of the organisation. For Tom Savage of Bright Green Talent 'You want to put people round you who make you feel good and work hard and are also willing to speak up as well and identify problems, too'.

Only appoint if you are 100% sure of the person. If you're not, it's better to start again, always.

Only appoint if you are 100% sure of the person. If you're not, it's better to start again, always. A word of warning: all our failed appointments have been people we have thought might 'develop into the job'. At best, people like that tend to take up a lot of your time. At worst, you end up having to let them go. If they don't feel right on day one, they will probably never feel right.

Once you've made your choice, get to work quickly. Immediately call the person (don't write!) and offer them the job. Tell them how impressed you were with them and how pleased you are to be making the offer. Remember, if they're good, they may have other options. Only when they've said 'yes' should you write to them confirming the offer.

I can hear some readers thinking, this is fine, but I don't have the time to do all this. Can I ask you, in response, if you have the time to deal with the consequences of making even one really poor appointment? Having done both, I know where I would rather invest my time.

Rob Harris of Advocacy Experience told me, 'There is an element of good practice in recruitment that is easy to apply but it guarantees nothing'. He feels that luck plays a major part and always will. But, when he's found the right person, Rob is very clear on how to motivate them. 'When you find a good person you respond to their needs at work; provide a career path, incentivise, give clarity and involve. Financial rewards always help – I don't subscribe to the "money doesn't motivate" argument – it's a form of currency the same as clarity and involvement.'

Views from the social entrepreneurs...

What do you look for in the people who work for you?

- 'Shared vision. Talents that complement my own and that add to the mix.' (Tim West, *Social Enterprise Magazine*)

- 'Rocco Forte said, "If you want good service hire nice people". It is critical in social care to get this right. Get it wrong and you have potential for abuse.' (Doug Cresswell, Pure Innovations)

- 'Enthusiasm, excellent references (anything less than excellent usually tells its own story).' (Rob Harris, Advocacy Experience)

- 'To be flexible, love what they do, believe in what they do.' (Luljeta Nuzi, Shpresa)

- 'Hard work, independence of mind, determination, willingness to make decisions and live with them.' (Steve Sears, ECT Group)

- 'People who bring something that bit different from me and from colleagues already in the organisation.' (Jonathan Senker, Advocacy Partners)

- 'The right skills, attitude and behaviour to do the job. I'm also a great believer in the transferability of cross-sector skills.' (Hannah Eyres, Keyfund)

Promoting equal opportunities and diversity

It is not only morally right that your new organisation is open to all and reflective of its community, it is also important to its success. You must make sure you're not just recruiting to type (namely, your type, whatever that is). Look at most organisations and you'll know what I mean by this.

> *Every organisation should reflect the nature of our society, not just a narrow sub-set. If possible, it should be particularly open to the groups you're working to benefit.*

Lots of research now shows that a diverse workforce will be much more effective than a monoculture in which everyone is, for example, white, female and over 50. Every organisation should reflect the nature of our society, not just a narrow sub-set. If possible, it should be particularly open to the groups you're working to benefit.

The way to do this is to make visible efforts. Disabled interviewers make a big statement to any disabled candidate. So, too, does a written commitment to interview all disabled people who fit the job spec. Avoid token gestures such as interview questions along the lines of 'How would you ensure equal opportunities if you were appointed to this post?'

Induction

So, they're here, in post. A good start is important. Induction tells people what and who they need to know and makes them feel at home as quickly as possible. It also helps to quell the anxiety people feel when they start a new job.

Allow a full month for induction. During that time the message should be clear: 'We don't expect much out of you in terms of your work but we do expect you to learn what you need to know about the organisation'. The new starter should have a busy month visiting projects and learning about services and becoming familiar with the environment and the sector.

An induction should include:
- the history and mission of your organisation;
- meeting colleagues and key customers or partners;
- learning about the sector within which you work;
- understanding internal processes (e.g. how to submit an expense claim);
- the expectations of the organisation.

I have seen so many organisations skimp on the induction only to find that people trip up later, or that people, six months into the job, still say they are finding their feet.

Managing and developing staff

> *Management is nothing more than motivating other people.*
> Lee Iacocca, American manager and writer

Easy to say, difficult to do. After all, as Tim West of *Social Enterprise Magazine* told me, 'Keeping them motivated means you can't be your chaotic, socially entrepreneurial self – you need to be organised, clear with your schedules, aims and requirements; you need to remember to tell them they are doing a fantastic job; you need to have clear salary progression, career progression and incentives. Most important, give them ownership of what you need them to do'. For Servane Mouazan of Ogunte 'It's a long relationship-building process'.

Back in the early days, Speaking Up had a particularly big problem. We couldn't manage staff very well. As a consequence, we never really knew how well they were doing and had no way of improving their skills. Training budgets didn't exist. Supervision was hit and miss. Slowly but surely our results dipped. More people expressed unhappiness at work. More people left the organisation in search of better things.

Since then we've come a long way. Our work is nationally recognised. People are happier now at work than ever. Our retention of staff is unusually high. People generally feel valued and supported. Here are some if the things we've done that have made a difference:

Supervision

All the research says that supervision leaves people more motivated and confident in what they're doing. I reckon, anecdotally, that good supervision makes a 20% difference to most people's performance. That's worth an extra day a week. All this for an investment of a couple of days per month.

When we were small, supervision meant a chat over coffee when we could fit it in. Now it is a semi-structured, recorded meeting for each employee on a monthly basis, covering the following questions:

- How's the work going?
- What's your progress against this year's (written, pre-agreed) goals?
- Is anything preventing you from performing at your best?
- How are you doing in the job?
- What can we do to help you to become even better at your job or happier at work?
- What are your next action points?

Each meeting should last a couple of hours. It should consist of 80% them talking and 20% you talking. It's their space. Notes of key points should be written up and then kept safe. See page 136 for more on supervision.

As a social entrepreneur, you are not likely to be the world's most natural people manager.

As a social entrepreneur, you are not likely to be the world's most natural people manager. People will find you visionary and inspirational but also find that you glaze over when it comes to detail.

If this is you, it is vital that one of your first appointments is somebody who loves managing and supporting people. My breakthrough came when I appointed a former social worker to look after our people. This cost money we didn't have, but it probably saved a lot more in the long run. I can date our improvement from the day she started.

That said, you should always supervise the two or three senior people immediately around you, whatever your size. These people are your arms, your legs and your voice. Therefore you have to invest in them, even when you'd rather be out networking!

Performance management

Good management consists of showing average people how to do the work of superior people...

John D. Rockefeller, American industrialist

This is something we aren't always that good at in the third sector, because what we do isn't always that easy to measure. But, without too much hard work, we can set up simple systems for rating the work we do and giving people a better idea of how well they are performing.

At Speaking Up, we use a simple 'traffic lights' system to rate our projects and services. This can work both for individuals and teams and is a great way to compare how you're doing in different parts of your new organisation.

We use traffic lights to rate:
- **Impact** – Do we have evidence of outcomes showing that we are making a difference to people's lives?
- **Management** – Are managers working to the standard we need them to?
- **Processes** – Do we have sound processes and are we using them?
- **Efficiency** – Is this person or team efficient in the way they use their time?
- **Relationships** – Does this person or team enjoy good relationships internally and externally?
- **Users** – Are users happy with our services?
- **Culture** – Does this person or team share our attitudes and values?
- **Development** – Does this person or team take this seriously?
- **Sickness** – How much time off does this person or team take?
- **Energy** – How much energy and passion does this person or team display?

Services are 'traffic-lighted' every quarter, which means their progress can be tracked over time. The ratings also give the people running them a clear message about what is expected and what most needs to be improved. Promotion is tied into strong ratings so everyone has to pay attention to them.

For some more hints on performance, see page 136.

Annual 360-degree appraisal

A 360-degree appraisal is one of the most powerful tools in the box. The benefits are the same as those of supervision but written large. It's a chance for serious reflection on how the work is going, how the person is getting on and what could be better.

It's called '360', because it contains contributions from others in the organisation. Ensure these are anonymous if you want them to be frank. Up to 10 people fill in a short form and e-mail it back. You then go through them during the meeting.

Most people find the appraisal process to be uplifting and re-motivating. It's a chance to acknowledge what's gone well, something that can get lost in the day to day operation of the organisation. It's also a chance to get a 'helicopter' view of the last year and the year ahead. Finally, it gives people a chance to reflect on the big question of their own overall development. There's more on annual appraisals on page 136.

My own appraisals have been very instructive. I now know beyond doubt what people see as my particular strengths, weaknesses and contributions. They have also given me areas to work on. Again, it's a very good investment of a day of your time.

Developing staff

In the start-up years of your new venture, there isn't much time or money for developing your people. This is forgivable for the first couple of years. But beyond that you've got to get this established, especially as you'll need many of them to take on new responsibilities as you grow.

As Speaking Up matured we went about this in two main ways:

- **Individual training budgets** – We invite staff to spend these on conferences, training, books or travel to other organisations.
- **Personal development plans (PDPs)** – We like our people to be thinking three years ahead and a PDP is there to help them do this (see page 137).

Dealing with underperformance

Executives owe it to the organisation and to their fellow workers not to tolerate non-performing individuals in important jobs.

Peter Drucker, management writer

Underperformance is a fact of life in many third sector organisations. It is often tolerated because dealing with it is bureaucratic and time consuming and not very nice work. As a result, charitable organisations end up resorting to other ways of dealing with it, such as restructuring. It is no coincidence that 13% of employment tribunals involve charities, while we employ only 5% of the workforce.

Since I started Speaking Up, I have personally been involved with about 12 people who were, in my view, seriously underperforming. It comes up as an issue at least twice a year – guaranteed.

The big message here has to be *deal with it*. Don't let it go unacknowledged. Poor performers are generally known and resented by others. One of the hardest parts of being the number one in an organisation is that you have to set an example here. If you duck it, so will everyone else.

So what do you do? The lessons of my experience are that underperformers have to be given the chance to improve. You should do this even when you feel, in your heart, that it's just not working out with someone. It's only fair.

This means raising the issues early, identifying clearly what you want to see improved and then checking weekly on progress, taking care to record all agreements. Raise the problems as factual issues, not something wrong with the person (even if you think the problem is actually a reflection of their character). Monitor the issue until either it has gone away or it is clear that it isn't going to be solved.

> *My recommendation to new social entrepreneurs is to put a high priority on making sure you comply with employment law.*

My recommendation to new social entrepreneurs is to put a high priority on making sure you comply with employment law. This sounds straightforward – who would deliberately flout the law? But it's remarkably easy to break the rules without realising it. One way is to subscribe to an employment law advice service. You pay a fee and, as long as you follow their advice to the letter during any issue, they will insure or indemnify you against any costs associated with legal action. These are flat-fee services and provide excellent value for money. (See page 137 for useful web links.) Until we grew to 90 staff, it was a useful substitute for having a human resources manager.

It is tempting, you may find, to take short cuts with problem people and use redundancies or restructuring to move people out, rather than go through due process. But I did this once and ended up in an employment tribunal. If you haven't attended one, it's pretty scary – a bit like appearing in court.

What to do if you get taken to an employment tribunal

If this ever happens (and it might), I strongly advise you to seek settlement through something called a 'no-fault' or 'compromise agreement'. Speak to an employment law adviser first, though.

An employment tribunal is a staggering drain on your time, energy and money. It will cost you a minimum of several thousand pounds to defend, plus your own time. Even if you win, you feel like you've lost. It is better to seek an agreement early on, even when you know someone's trying it on. Compromise agreements seldom come to more than the costs of defending a claim – unless the employee is claiming that they have experienced discrimination. It feels like admitting defeat if you haven't done anything wrong, but believe me, a compromise agreement is better than ending up in an employment tribunal.

Exit

Every year up to 20% of the people working for your new organisation will leave. This is natural and normal. Ideally, they will be leaving in a better position than they came in, having had a positive experience.

But this won't always be the case. Occasionally, they will be leaving due to a redundancy or they may have been sacked. On such occasions its vitally important that you handle people with care and that you comply with any legal obligations.

Occasionally, you will need to make a post redundant. For the occupier of the post this need not mean the end of their employment, as you may want to redeploy them elsewhere. But if you can't, you'll need to make provision for a redundancy.

Again, don't just rely on your common sense here. Redundancy is an area that is covered by detailed legislation. Failure to observe it can result in being taken to an employment tribunal.

Of particular importance are consultative meetings with the affected people and a process of informing people of your unfolding plans, giving them time to respond.

Whatever you do, make sure you are getting legal advice the whole way, either from an employment law advisor or lawyer.

Sack toxic people

Every so often you will unwittingly employ somebody who is 'toxic'. Vital signs of a toxic are a permanent negative attitude, total cynicism and a tendency to spread negativity to others. These people, in my experience, are fairly immune to the usual carrots and sticks. They don't change. If you end up with a toxic inside your organisation, my advice is to move heaven and earth to move them on – and fast. Undealt with, toxic behaviour will destroy your organisation faster than you can build it.

So what do you do? This sounds harsh, but you need to isolate toxic people. You do this by challenging their behaviour very directly and publicly. They, and everyone else, must know that toxic behaviour is not acceptable to you. Then you need to have a serious conversation about the future. It is possible to do this. We have, somehow or other, successfully moved on every single toxic we have encountered at Speaking Up – even if it has cost us money to do so. Call it an investment in the organisation!

How to create an organisation people love working for

Why is it that whenever I ask for a pair of hands, a brain comes attached?'
Henry Ford, American founder of Ford Motor Company

Henry Ford had one view of people – as pairs of hands to do a job. Yet we know that only when people *as people* are happy, engaged and passionate can they deliver their best work.

So how do we do this? Well, its simple – but hard too … You've got to give power away. Only by doing this can you unleash the level of creativity and motivation required to make people love what they do – and want to stay.

For you as a founder or CEO it means you stop making all the big calls and instead focus yourself on designing an organisation in which people can innovate, excel and contribute to the bottom lines of the organisation from wherever they work within it. My favourite management writer Gary Hamel, of London Business School puts it like this:

To enfranchise employees you have to disenfranchise managers.

What does this mean in practice? Organisations that command the respect of employees understand that people's number one need is to feel recognised and valued. This isn't just about money, though fair pay is important, it is about the way people interact, the kind of atmosphere that you create and the view you take of human potential.

I had to think long and hard about all of this a few years ago when it dawned on me that several of our people didn't feel positive about Speaking Up. By contrast, they felt ignored, unrecognised and devalued by me personally.

It forced a few changes. Making Speaking Up a place that people like to work at meant doing a few things really well.

1. **Listening to people** – People need to feel heard. Just look at all the books and blogs out there full of people's views about the world. Being heard is a big human need. Organisations also need to be places where people feel heard – not a variation on the military where you do as you are told end-of-matter. You don't always need to act on what you hear but you need to make people feel like they're being listened to. Spend time sharing your thoughts and plans with your people. They'll feel more committed to any eventual action if you do this.

2. **Celebrating success** – I am often surprised by the 'miserablism' of many third sector organisations, in which success often just goes unacknowledged. It is vital to get out the champagne whenever things go well. Human beings have marked success by celebration since the beginning of time; it makes sense to do this in our organisations.

3. **Improving our working environment** – Too many third sector staff work in third-rate settings. Studies show a clear relationship between happiness at work and productivity. Over time, Speaking Up has gone from one of the worst to a reasonably well-housed and well-equipped organisation. Don't underestimate the influence of environment on people's feelings about their jobs and employers.

4. **Being generous to staff** – People in charities and social businesses shouldn't have to pay for their own Christmas dinner! It's important in a sector where pay isn't good to have a 'recognition budget'. Small gestures like that tell staff you really value them. This budget adds up to a few thousand pounds a year. In terms of goodwill, it is an extremely efficient spend.

5. **Treating people as people** – Don't treat people as parts of a machine. It sounds simple but most workplaces, even in today's world, are a fairly rigid hierarchy in which we all have fixed tasks, roles and status – like Henry Ford's car plants over a century ago. While some kind of order is important, such hierarchy creates an illusion that all talent, wisdom and creativity resides at the 'top' while people at the 'bottom' just get on and do.

At Speaking Up we work hard to reduce the impact of hierarchy. Therefore, we go light on job titles, status symbols and so on. Nobody has their own office or company car. People dress as they like. Anyone can talk to anyone about anything – including their ideas. Groups drawn from across the organisation work on cross-organisational challenges, such as branding and human resources. Innovation is encouraged and sponsored from all levels.

How to empower people

On an everyday level, empowering people is about giving employees a much bigger say on a range of things:

- **Use of time** – Do people have some choice over their hours, their schedule and activities?
- **Goals** – Do you set goals for people or with them?

- **Recruitment** – Are you prepared to involve your staff in recruitment and allow them to choose their managers?
- **Rewards** – Are you prepared to involve everybody in determining levels of reward – including your own?
- **Budgets** – Are you happy to let people nearest to the coal-face set budgets and decide on changes in the way budgets are spent?
- **Outcomes** – Would you give employees responsibility for deciding which information to collect to prove your outcomes?
- **Innovation** – Do you create real opportunities for employees' ideas to shape the new things you are doing?
- **Strategy** – Could you turn over what the future of the company looks like to your employees?

Don't be worried if this isn't how your company looks now. Mine doesn't look like this either – not yet. But this is the way the most innovative and consistently successful companies in the world, such as Google, RM Gore and Semco are running their operations. They are turning their organisations into places that are run by their employees and in which the powers of managers are less those of direction and more those of facilitation. Employees at Google, for example, have a right to refuse to do something they are asked to do if they passionately feel that their time needs to be spent doing something different. Yes, its very different isn't it? That's 21st century management – you might as well start with it rather than try to play catch-up once you've set up your organisation along traditional top-down lines.

FINDING AND KEEPING THE BEST PEOPLE

Have you been giving the 'people' side of your business some serious thought?

Are you out of the start-up period and moving towards building a sustainable organisation, when this is even more important?

- Social entrepreneurs succeed only if they can create organisations that deliver the goods.
- It's a big cliché, but people are your biggest asset in delivering your services.
- People are also your biggest cost, so they deserve as much attention as anything else, if not more.

Flowers flourish when they are watered and shrivel up when they are not. People are no different.

Sir Richard Branson, founder of Virgin

9 Finding the right partners

Coming together is a beginning; keeping together is progress; working together is success.

Henry Ford, American founder of Ford Motor Company

In a sense, everything you do as a social entrepreneur will be a partnership – a partnership with your staff and volunteers, your paying customers and clients. The kinds of partnerships I want to look at now are strategic partnerships – major agreements between your organisation and others to work towards shared goals.

Partnerships are increasingly a feature of the way the world works. If you look at industries such as software or automobiles, many of the big companies collaborate as well as compete. If you buy a Ford, a Mazda or a Volvo, it will have the same chassis holding it together.

Partnership and collaboration is happening more in the third sector too. Indeed, the recent success of Speaking Up has been built on a highly successful partnership with venture philanthropy charity, Impetus Trust. However, it is important to get into the right partnerships and on the right terms. This chapter aims to help you think about partnership opportunities and make the right calls when deciding whether to work alone or with others.

What is a partnership?

At its simplest, a partnership is a relationship between two or more independent organisations. It is freely entered into for the purpose of achieving shared goals. A partnership is often sustained for a period of years and is, in this sense, a big strategic decision.

What reasons might prompt your venture to go into partnership with other organisations?

- **To achieve major ambitions** – If you have a big vision, often it won't be possible to achieve it alone. You need to work with others to make it happen. Partnerships can be the perfect vehicle. For Speaking Up, partnering with the Impetus Trust enabled us to triple the number of people we worked with, grow to a national scale and become more sustainable. For the Impetus Trust, the partnership also enabled them to prove to their stakeholders that their model of venture philanthropy would work in a UK setting.
- **To share risks** – Sometimes a project can be desirable but could also bring you down if it fails. Sharing this risk with another organisation is a way to achieve the task yet reduce the chances of damage to your enterprise. With

the Impetus Trust, we shared the risks around sudden expansion and this enabled us to take audacious steps into new markets, which otherwise would not have been possible.

- **To bring skills on board** – Our goals often require skills and know-how we don't have in house. A partnership can secure the key elements and enable you to gain a deeper understanding of those skills yourself. Our partnership with the Impetus Trust introduced business know-how, which, until then, didn't exist in our organisation.
- **To help users** – Sometimes partnerships are necessary for users or customers. It can be hard for users to navigate all the independent organisations that can help them. Equally, a funder may prefer not to deal with five single organisations in a sector but with a partnership of all.
- **To raise money or win contracts** – This is a very common reason for going into partnership. A coalition of organisations can present a much sought-after holistic approach, something that separate bids can seldom achieve. Speaking Up has used this several times to obtain European funding.

At Speaking Up and in other ventures I've had experience of a number of partnerships, all motivated by different reasons. Overall, while some have absorbed inordinate amounts of energy and achieved very little, our biggest and most important partnership (Impetus) has transformed the organisation.

Good and bad partnership – two stories

Good partnership

Let me tell you the story of the Impetus Trust partnership. In 2002, Speaking Up was an award-winning local charity with a problem. A big problem. Despite our success and future potential, we were sinking fast. We hadn't created a sustainable organisation. We depended on grants for 85% of our income and these didn't cover all our costs. Our aspiration to triple the number of people with whom we worked was a pipe dream. A step change was required but we lacked capacity to do this. The only answer was to develop new income streams, but to do so we needed money and advice.

Our partnership with the Impetus Trust enabled us to invest in new services and improve the infrastructure of the organisation. This meant an investment of £400,000 and a major infusion of advice in key areas such as marketing, branding and measurement of outcomes. Four years on, our turnover has moved from £500,000 to £3 million per year and beneficiary numbers have trebled. From Impetus Trust's point of view, we are one of their most successful investment partners.

Bad partnership

LEAP was the name of a partnership between about 10 local charities aimed at obtaining EU funding for employment programmes. One of the charities, the largest, was set up to be 'lead partner'. Speaking Up agreed to join in because the money seemed reasonable, the aims were on-mission and we didn't need to carry the risk of dealing directly with the demanding funders at the EU. However, LEAP was soon in trouble. Targets were being missed by the less efficient partners. Furthermore, some felt that others were not pulling their weight. The lead partner soon realised they had made a mistake in carrying so much risk and, quite understandably, their enthusiasm waned. The finances quickly started to go wrong. Meetings to sort out the mess became long, bad-tempered events. Partners were soon finding the time and energy costs associated with LEAP far outweighed the financial benefits. The partnership ended after two years with the lead partner losing tens of thousands of pounds as well as its previously good relationships with smaller partners.

LEAP was a 'paper' partnership, cobbled together very quickly against tight deadlines as a means to obtain money for the participants. A partnership group was put together, which included every single organisation, all of whom had to approve each decision. Little thought had gone into the best way to manage it and how to make it effective. It was the classic 'toxic partnership'.

What makes a good partnership?

In my experience, a good partnership has six principal qualities:

1. **The benefits to all organisations are very clear and unambiguous** – Both the Impetus Trust and Speaking Up had a lot to gain from successful collaboration. With LEAP, it wasn't really clear from the start whether the partnership would be a good thing. If you're going to enter a partnership, it needs to feel by far the best option.

2. **The decision-making methods for the partnership are efficient** – The Impetus Trust and Speaking Up sat down every month and made decisions together on key issues. Once decided, things happened. With LEAP, decision making was torturously slow and often agreements were not honoured.

3. **Roles and deliverables within the partnership are agreed upfront and written down** – From the off, the Impetus Trust and Speaking Up had a written agreement about what could be expected and what would happen if either side failed to deliver. LEAP lacked any clear process if any partner failed to fulfil its commitments.

4. **The benefits and risks within the partnership are fairly spread between partners** – With the Impetus Trust, this felt clear and fair on both sides. With LEAP, the lead agency (not us, thankfully) carried by far the most risk. They ended up out of pocket and understandably angry.

5. **Meetings and paperwork are sensible** – Our meetings with the Impetus Trust were monthly one-to-one sessions with a yearly review attended by our respective Chairs. One piece of paper kept track of developments. LEAP meetings involved up to 12 people for half a day each month and involved an extraordinary level of paperwork.

6. **People in the partnership actually enjoy working together and trust one another** – Working relations with Impetus were always harmonious and honest. LEAP contained people with long-held antipathies. Meetings were always pretty dire.

What is a partner?

When you're looking for partners, it is worth distinguishing between three different types:

- **Consultant partner** – committed to being available for their guidance.
- **Member partner** – committed to having a limited input.
- **Core member** – committed to giving most time compared to consultant or member partners.

Finding partners

> *The poor man who enters into a partnership with one who is rich makes a risky venture.*
>
> Titus Maccius Plautus, Roman playwright

Usually, while a partnership project is being developed, ideas are shared between a couple of organisations; but that may not be enough. The project probably needs more partners. Looking for partners requires thinking about who would be interested in your planned service and what it could offer:

- Who could make good potential partners?
- Who else offers what you do?
- What other organisations are involved in helping your client group?
- Which organisations could do more by adding your services or location as a base for their work?
- Which organisations could help you in planning the different aspects of your services?

Building the partnership

One approach I really like is this ten-step partnership management process[1] summarising how to identify and work best with partners:

---

[1] Taken from Charles Lines. His material can be found at www.tallistraining.co.uk/partnership%20tips.htm.

Step 1 – What is the purpose?
■ Define the purpose of the potential partnership.
■ Define what needs to be achieved.
■ Decide what outcomes are required.

Step 2 – Can a partnership provide what is needed?
■ Is working in partnership *definitely* the best way to achieve the above purpose and outcomes?
■ What skills, expertise, support and overall added effectiveness do you need from working in partnership?

List the potential gains and drawbacks from partnership working. If the gains clearly outweigh the drawbacks, carry on with this process. If the drawbacks outweigh the gains, reconsider.

Step 3 – Who are the potential partners out there?
Identify all potential partners from the Stakeholder Day – resist making judgements about their relative importance or suitability.

Step 4 – Who are the major 'core' partners?
■ Which of the above partners will help to maximise the gains and minimise the drawbacks?
■ Where is the shared interest with each partner and where do interests converge and diverge?
■ What is the positive pay-off for each partner?

Remember that small numbers of partners are better than many. When making the selection, remember that credibility and powerful sponsorship are important for effective partnership working.

Step 5 – Which structure best meets the partnership's needs?
Which of the following structures will best help realise potential gains and best suit all the partners?
■ a project structure
■ a permanent structure such as joint-venture CIC

Remember that different partners may need to be dealt with in different ways and that the type of structure that the partnership needs may change during its lifetime.

Step 6 – What does the partnership need from stakeholders?
Consider each stakeholder in turn and ask the following types of questions:
■ Who wants the partnership to succeed?
■ Who wants it to fail?
■ Who is offering support?

- Whose support is necessary?
- Who is offering resources?

Step 7 – What is the best way to manage each stakeholder?
Think about the stakeholders in the following terms:
- Which stakeholders have high interest in the partnership and high power in terms of their ability to positively or adversely affect it?
- Which stakeholders have high interest but low power?
- Which have low interest but high power?
- Which have low interest and low power?

Step 8 – How can the partnership contract for success?
- Jointly identify and agree some significant quick wins.
- Jointly identify and agree key areas not suitable for quick wins that need special attention.
- Create an agreed action plan that clearly shows which partner is responsible for what and gives agreed deadlines. Agree review dates for each action point, especially where the outcome to be achieved is long term or ongoing.
- Make sure that your contract for success addresses both the outputs expected from the partnership and how the partnership is going to work together to achieve them.
- Make sure that complete tasks are allocated to partners.

Step 9 – How can the partnership make the most of partners' cultures/ways of working?
- What types of organisational cultures do the partners come from? How are they used to working?
- Consider each partner in turn. How can most be made of the strengths of each partner's culture and how can weaknesses be minimised?

Step 10 – How can the partnership audit its ongoing effectiveness?
Ask the following types of questions:
- Is the purpose still clear and current?
- Do all partners buy into the purpose and into the partnership's structure and processes?
- Are all partners still needed? Are new partners needed?
- Do stakeholders know what is going on and are they being managed appropriately?
- Have all partners co-created/agreed the outcomes and their success indicators?
- Does the partnership know the costs incurred and do the benefits realised justify these costs?

FINDING THE RIGHT PARTNERS

Partnerships – are you for or against them?

When it comes to building partnerships, are you getting a clear message about what's at stake?

- Look before you leap. Ask the right questions. The reason a lot of organisations get mired in ineffective and wasteful partnerships is because they fail to ask the right questions at the right time.
- Understand the costs and benefits for your organisation.
- Most partnership invitations will not actually be a good idea, so approach each one in a cool-headed way.
- It's really important for you to walk away if something doesn't offer your venture clear benefits.
- For partnerships to be worth all the meetings, negotiation, liaison and consensus-building, they need, in my experience, to deliver not in teaspoons but in bucket loads.

By the time a partnership dissolves, it has dissolved.

John Updike, American author

10 Keeping on top of the money

Business is not financial science, it's about trading ... buying and selling. It's about creating a product or service so good that people will pay for it.
Dame Anita Roddick, founder of The Body Shop

Success or failure, even in charities and social businesses, often comes down to how well you manage your money. I have seen several new ventures fold and the inability to manage money has always been a feature (though not the only problem) in all of them. Conversely, successful organisations tend to have their finances well under control. Setting up a new enterprise means that, whether you like it or not, you're going to have to get intimately involved in finance. And if you're like me and have little interest or confidence in managing money, this chapter is aimed at you.

The chapter splits into three sections. The first section tells you the real basics of what you need in place as you start your new venture. The second goes through, in very basic terms, the simple control processes required to keep a grip on your finances. The third section looks at the financial aspects of employing people. Along the way are some top finance tips from myself and others who have set up charities and social businesses. And, finally, I signpost you to useful resources that tackle each specific aspect of managing your finances.

Getting started

When I set up Speaking Up, I got a lot of things wrong. First of all, I didn't record income and outgoings very often – every three months at best. I had little idea of how much cash we had in the bank or whether it was enough to pay our bills. I was forever losing invoices and receipts. I often forgot to pay invoices, meaning we got a lot of angry letters demanding payment. I also failed to check our bank statements against our monthly accounts, so I would never have known if cheques had bounced or if money was missing.

The reason all this happened was that I was too busy doing everything else. And, if I am honest, I didn't quite understand how to organise some of the basics. In hindsight, I was lucky not to have sent Speaking Up into insolvency. While this sounds really irresponsible – and it was – I know lots of entrepreneurial people who, early on, lost a grip of their finances. I eventually found a freelance book-keeper to organise mine for me.

So what basics do you need to have in place?

A bank account

In the first place you need to choose a bank account. Ideally, you need a bank that is easy to deal with and understands, on some level, what you are doing. When I started, hardly any banks would let me have an account with them! Today, most high street banks cater for people setting up either charities or social firms. Factors to consider when choosing a bank account are:

- the level of bank charges (don't pay for a current account!);
- whether or not you need an overdraft facility;
- whether they offer interest on current accounts;
- whether they will give you an overdraft and at what cost.

The very best accounts also enable your money to work for you outside business hours. What happens, in effect, is that the funds are swept out of your account overnight, put to work in financial markets on the other side of the world and returned, with interest, in the morning. All while you sleep. You will, however, want to be sure that your bank uses such funds ethically. There is little point in your money effecting positive social change here, only for it to be causing social damage 'over there'!

Your cash book

While I managed for a couple of years without one, I was, without realising it, playing with fire. This is your single most important piece of financial record-keeping. It records all of the payments into and out of your business' bank account. It is crucial to set up the book as soon as you start your charity or social business. The cash book doesn't have to be a physical book. In fact you'd be best equipped with a PC package such as Quickbooks, which enables you to record all transactions and does all the calculations for you. Fail to keep one, as I did, and there's a much bigger chance of your going bust, getting ripped off or, worst of all, being accused of fiddling the books.

Sales invoice file

This is where you keep all the invoices that you send out to customers or funders. This file is both helpful for your record-keeping and for reassuring anyone auditing your books. You should keep your sales invoices in a file, in strict numerical order and divide them up into the months of the year. Unpaid invoices should be kept in a special section at the front of the file until they have been settled. At this point, you should mark them paid and place them in the appropriate month. You should chase up any unpaid invoices quickly – in person, if necessary.

Purchase invoice file

This records all the invoices you receive from others asking for payment. This needs to be a physical file with a divider for each month and a front section for your own unpaid bills. On receiving an invoice, place it in the 'unpaid' section until it's paid. Then remove it and place it under the appropriate month in which you made the payment.

How do you control your finances?

You have a number of important financial control processes at your disposal. Ideally, while you need to understand how these processes work, you should pay a freelance book-keeper to do it for you. It's a superb investment because it takes a lot of time to learn in detail how to do all of these things – time you could be spending building your new venture.

Bank reconciliation statement

'Reconciliation' between the cash book and the bank statement simply means explaining the differences. Differences between the cash book and the bank statement can arise from:

- Timing of payments. There is often a delay between you paying an invoice or banking a cheque and it showing in your accounts;
- Error at the bank;
- Delays in payments reaching their destination;
- Failure of whoever receives your payment to put it in the bank;
- Fraud.

The reconciliation statement simply traces the difference between what is in your cash book and what your bank account says.

A bank reconciliation statement enables you to make sure that transactions recorded are mirrored in the bank statement. This is particularly important if several people are involved in managing the finances. Should any money go 'missing', this should show up in a monthly bank reconciliation. Even if you're doing it all yourself, it is reassuring to funders and trustees to know you do a bank reconciliation statement each month.

Budgets

Believe it or not, I ran Speaking Up for two years without actually writing a budget. This was partly because a lot of it was in my head. But this is a dangerous game – a budget is the main tool you have to control your finances.

At its simplest, a budget is a plan of all your income and spending during a particular year. Much of what will be in the expenditure side of your budget can easily and quite accurately be planned. The income side often isn't so easy, because you may not know exactly what is coming in. However, you should be able to identify what you hope will come in over the course of a year.

Once you have constructed a budget it is important to update it in the light of developments in the business. Variations between actual and expected income and expenditure can be compared. This will show up trends in the organisation at a fairly early stage. If you're doing well, you'll be able to expand your spending or investment at the earliest possible time. Conversely, if things aren't looking good, you can pare back some spending before you hit a crisis.

'Profit and loss' account

The 'P and L' is one of the three principal business reporting and measuring tools (along with the balance sheet and cash flow statement). The P and L is essentially a trading account for a period, usually a year. But it can also be created monthly and cumulatively or 'year-to-date'. The P and L typically shows sales revenues, cost of sales/cost of goods sold, a gross profit or loss margin (sometimes called 'contribution'), fixed overheads and or operating expenses, and then a profit before tax figure (PBT). Basically, the P and L shows how well the company has performed in its trading activities.

The monthly P and L accounts provide a snapshot of the financial position at the end of each month. The accounts list the actual income and spending against your budgeted income and spending. This will determine whether you are in profit or loss – surplus or deficit – on the month just gone.

The variances against budget are often easily explained – outgoings and income are often delayed for all sorts of reasons. But variances can also indicate problems such as a big over-spend or a customer who has hit hard times. If you can't explain and deal with variances between your budget and monthly accounts, you are far more likely to get into financial trouble.

Cash flow statement

Cash flow problems dog many small organisations. In fact, many businesses end up in real trouble not because they don't have customers – but because they can't manage the flow of cash in and out of the business.

A cash flow statement answers the questions 'What money is coming into the business?' and 'What money is leaving the business?' It is one of the most important pieces of financial information you need, particularly if you are new and there is some delay between your expenditure and expected income.

A cash flow problem arises when your need for cash cannot be matched by what you have available to you. You may have £10,000 due to come in next month but if you owe £5,000 in unpaid national insurance, you may find yourself in a position where you are effectively insolvent. This happens to thousands of businesses every year.

The first step in managing cash flow is to create a cash flow statement. This is a broken-down version of your budget, which states, each month, how much cash is entering and leaving the organisation. This way you can predict your cash position month by month or even week by week if necessary. Once you know this, you can foresee when problems might arise during the year and make provision for this. You could, for example, ask for a temporary overdraft if you know that a big payment will be due in a particular month or ask all your creditors for a bit longer to pay them. A clear and credible cash flow statement helps to convince banks and creditors that you can actually pay them and you're not going to default on any arrangement.

Balance sheet

The balance sheet is one of the three essential measurement reports for the performance and health of a company, along with the P and L and the cash flow statement. The balance sheet is a 'snapshot' in time of the how the assets of the company are made up. It tells you how much is held in cash, how much is owed by creditors and what the physical assets are worth. It also tells you where the assets in a company came from.

If, say, you were looking at taking over a charity or company, a balance sheet is where to look for information about their debts, the amount of debt they might have in relation to what they actually own, their reserves, their physical assets, the amount of cash in the organisation and, if the business is privately owned, the 'book' value of the shares held in the company.

Employing staff

Sooner or later, it is likely that you'll need to take people on as employees. The New Employer's Starter Pack helps you through the process of taking on a new employee. It contains all of the forms, tables and other information you need in order to:

- record a new employee's details;
- calculate an employee's income tax, national insurance contributions (NICs) and any student loan deductions, so that you can make the correct deductions on payday;
- calculate the employer's NICs;
- keep a record of all payments and deductions.

It also contains the forms that you'll need if a new employee doesn't have a P45, or doesn't know their national insurance number. Some forms and documents are included in paper format, but others will be in electronic format on the starter pack CD-Rom.

Enclosed with the starter pack will be your employer reference number. Make sure you keep this – you'll need to use it on official forms and correspondence. To get a starter pack, call the HM Revenue & Customs (HMRC) New Employers helpline on 0845 60 70 143. As well as sending the starter pack, staff at the helpline will be able to answer any immediate queries you may have.

KEEPING ON TOP OF THE MONEY

Are you ready to do what it takes to keep on top of the money?

Are you ready to delegate the creation of your P and L, bank reconciliation, cash flow and balance sheet to a book-keeper?

- Like it or not, the money side of your business really needs your attention.
- Put a day aside a month to analyse your finances.
- Make it your business to eliminate any variances between budgeted and actual income.
- Only include expected income within a budget, not fantasy income. Update your budget forecast in line with expectations of income and expenditure. Guess what? Things change.

Good finance is at the heart of a successful business, So don't fear it, embrace it.

Mike Southon and Chris West, authors of 'The Beermat Entrepreneur'

11 Governance: building a board of trustees and directors

Nearly all men can stand adversity, but if you want to test a man's character, give him power.
Abraham Lincoln, American President 1861–5

Unless you own the company outright, like Rob Harris or Miles Hanson do, you will share the power over your new organisation with other people. For an entrepreneur, this can feel tough, or even unnatural. If, like me and many of the other entrepreneurs featured here, your organisation is now a charity, you may well cede all formal power to people who weren't necessarily with you at the start.

This can be a real challenge. For it is the board of directors, not you, who is responsible for overall strategy and direction. Even more of a challenge is when the board lacks the capacity to do this well. The challenge for you as a new entrepreneur, as it was for me at Speaking Up, will be to fill that gap, while finding a board that is up to the task.

One of our panel, Owen Jarvis of Aspire Support UK, puts it like this: 'You need a small but highly committed and able board who really have something to offer and are going to get their sleeves rolled up. And if they are any good that means being very supportive of the founder entrepreneur while things are being road-tested. But it also means being a great critical friend. Don't appoint people to give you an easy ride and don't ask for one.'

How a board can add value

I would concur with Owen's point – that a good board should help you get to places you can't get to on your own, quickly and on time. But, as a social entrepreneur, you may find that a board of directors can feel like a bit of an inconvenience. That's certainly how I felt during our early years. Decisions had to be deferred, sometimes for weeks, only for board members not to turn up or not to have read their papers. I also had people on my board who, despite their good intentions, didn't have business minds and got bogged down in minutiae. Again, it can be very frustrating when it is they, not you, who ultimately carry legal responsibility for the organisation.

However, over time, as my board improved, I became convinced of its value to the organisation. Other social entrepreneurs feel that a board is of real use to them so long as the chemistry is right. For Nick Temple of School for Social Entrepreneurs 'there is a fine balance to be struck between having people aligned with the mission, and people who provide challenging, robust feedback. Or, in shorthand, don't pack your board with all your friends, but don't pack it with potential enemies either'.

A really good board will add value to your venture in a number of ways:

- **Individual board members will have expertise in a number of areas useful to the venture and can be called upon to advise when needed** – I have easy access to a financial controller in a large pharmaceutical company, the former CEO of a major UK charity, a successful local businesswoman and an emerging social entrepreneur who has career-switched from the City. Together, these people are a significant resource – one which, today, I couldn't do without.
- **Some board members will have superb contacts and networks that can help** – One of my chairs (I have two co-chairs) has one of the best address books I have seen. This means that making new contacts is a lot easier than it would be on my own.
- **It can be a brilliant sounding board for new ideas and a check on any bad ones coming from you or your management team** – Disabled people occupy six of the twelve seats on my board and are always on hand when I need to know whether Speaking Up's ideas will strike a chord with this social group.
- **The board can provide you with important support for what you're seeking to achieve** – As the leader of a venture, I have always needed people around me who believed in what I was doing. My board has formed an important part of my support network.
- **The chair of a board is an ideal strategic partner for you as CEO** – I have two chairs and our monthly meetings provide a wonderful space for reflection and debate about long-term direction.

Balance is a factor in the minds of many social entrepreneurs. Nick Temple again: 'I would recommend a board with a good mix of skills and experience, who understand you as a person as much as the organisation, and include users/beneficiaries of the service where possible: they keep it real'.

Surveys by NCVO and others have found that capacity is a problem for most trustee boards. According to the Association of Chief Executives of Voluntary Organisations (ACEVO), the biggest issue on their helpline for CEOs is problems with the chairs or board members.

So this is tricky and will be for you, too, unless, of course, you actually own the business you set up. My own approach to board development has been to get personally involved in the recruitment of board members. As a paid member of staff you're not officially supposed to drive this yourself. However, I have yet to meet the CEO of a small organisation who doesn't. This way you can 'cherry-pick' people who might be suitable to avoid having unsuitable candidates signing up as directors and becoming stuck with them. This sounds crude, but that's sometimes how it has to be.

Recruiting trustees and directors

So how do you recruit good trustees and directors? Research shows that there is a shortage of trustees in the UK, mainly because of misconceptions about the risks involved; people feel they are putting themselves on the line financially. Furthermore, trusteeship is not a paid role. If you are a busy chairperson putting in a day a week, this can feel rough. Finding people who really want to do the job isn't easy. Organisations are increasingly writing 'job descriptions' for trustees and recruiting openly in the press. I do it and I recommend you to do the same.

An ideal board will contain the following mix of expertise:
- **Finance skills** – Ideally, your treasurer will be somebody who comes from a finance background and can read and understand audited accounts. Mine is a financial controller of a plc.
- **User experience** – The people who experience the kind of life that is typical of your user group need to be represented. As a social business, it is important, if you can, to ensure this happens. It keeps users at the heart and soul of your organisation.
- **Human resources (HR) skills** – It is useful to have a board member with a background in HR to advise and support you on staff problems. This becomes more important as you employ more people. Someone who has filled an HR role is ideal, although anyone with a management qualification is likely to be able to help.
- **Public relations (PR) skills** – Getting known is a major challenge for new organisations and it is useful to have someone on board to advise you on attracting the right kind of public attention. I have never found such a person, but charities that have, such as Kids Company, have benefited enormously from this.
- **Senior management skills** – It is important to have one person on your board who can oversee the development of the organisation in terms of the way it is managed and run. Having the former CEO of national charity, Mencap, on my board has been an unquestioned asset.
- **Entrepreneurial skills** – As a social entrepreneur, you need to have like-minded people on the board, somebody who forces the board to be enthusiastic about new ideas and encouraging of taking risks. I headhunted two entrepreneurs, one commercial and one social, to provide this kind of input. These two people are a constant challenge to the rest of the board – and to me.

Perhaps the most important director will be your chair. The chairperson/social entrepreneur relationship can make or break your fledgling organisation. I have been very lucky with all of mine. Each chair has recognised my special role as a founder and supported my vision, rather than try to impose their own. This doesn't always happen, though, so you need to be very careful when seeking a chairperson, particularly if you choose to become a charity. It's also vital to find someone who is made of the right stuff. Owen Jarvis puts it very well indeed: 'Social enterpreneurs need an active and engaged chair who can get their teeth into both social and business agendas. Tea and biscuits in church halls this is not – it's a serious business – social enterprise is not a revamp of comfy charitable activities. It is a new era'. Owen's implication – that you need a serious business mind as chair, not simply a well-wisher – is a good one.

Julie Stokes of Winston's Wish points to the real gains to be made from a fruitful relationship with a chair. She has had the same chair since foundation. She says, 'We are like chalk and cheese in some ways but it is a very respectful and loyal relationship, which I value enormously. Her advice is always considered and clear with a superb appreciation of governance issues (not my forte). I also believe that her experience of having confidently run several organisations herself brings a level of understanding on the boundaries between the two roles, which has worked well'.

What to do if your board is weak

The main thing is not to panic. It is not the end of the world. In reality, many organisations are run by their senior management teams, particularly early on. I ran Speaking Up single-handedly for several years until my board got up to speed. While you need to seriously commit to playing a role in improving your board, it is unlikely, in the short term, that your venture will fail due to a weak board. However, this becomes a bigger risk in the medium and long term, which is why it must be addressed. Indeed, had we not evenyually got our board into shape, I doubt we would have inspired the confidence of so many partners and funders.

There are three main problems associated with a weak board:
- There is a lack of advice when you need it. I recall several times, particularly early on, when I needed guidance and had nowhere to go.
- You often find that the board is preoccupied with the wrong issues and a conservatism borne out of not really understanding what is going on. This is very common on boards. The result is that people feel insecure and just refuse to take decisions.
- Interference in staff and management roles is relatively common, particularly in smaller organisations in which trustees are also working as volunteers. I have experienced this several times and, on occasion, I still do.

So what are the solutions? Before my board was strong enough to help me sufficiently, I sought advice from mentors and advisers external to the board. One or two eventually joined as trustees. Training for board members really helps them to understand their role better, and excellent trustee training is now available online ('Trustee Driving Licence' from NCVO, www.ncvo-vol.org.uk).

Finally, an induction for trustees into the work of the organisation and regular updates from staff on what's happening gives trustees the confidence and insight to do a better job of overseeing the work.

IT'S THE
BORED OF
DIRECTORS

Governance in charities

If your new venture becomes a charity (as 64% of social enterprises now are), you'll need to turn your board of directors into a trustee board. Unfortunately, if you're also employed by the venture, you can't normally be a trustee. This is because charitable status brings with it a forced split between a non-executive board and a paid management to whom it delegates responsibility for delivery. This happened to me. To many social entrepreneurs, this type of arrangement can feel intuitively wrong. Here you are, you've set up a new venture from nothing and now you are excluded from its governance. If you want any of the benefits associated with having charitable status, however, that is the way it is.

GOVERNANCE: BUILDING A BOARD OF TRUSTEES AND DIRECTORS

Are you coming to the conclusion that, for social entrepreneurs, there are no easy answers on governance issues?

Charitable or non-charitable?

- You may need to lead the recruitment of a strong board of directors and trustees.
- A strong board gives you connections, support, credibility and on-hand expertise.
- In a perfect world, superb governance will help you to realise your dream. The reality is often somewhat different. You just have to work around the issues with the people on your board, and gradually get the mix right.

When you have exhausted all the possibilities, remember this – you haven't.

Thomas Edison, inventor of the light bulb

12 From baby to child: dealing with your growing pains

Passion is the element in which we live; without it, we vegetate.
Lord Byron, English poet

When you start your new venture, you run on passion. The venture is your new baby. It's small, it's full of energy and everyone involved is feeling the same way. There's very little formal hierarchy and you all take turns to clean the office! There's a lot of shared laughter and quite a few tears.

This is exactly what it was like in the first couple of years of Speaking Up. In such an environment, structure, processes, policies and systems don't matter all that much. Neither does basic infrastructure like a nice office and a decent photocopier. Our love of what we were doing blinded us to these shortcomings.

The lack of structure during the baby years gave us a big advantage in terms of speed. This period without structure or processes was the most creative phase in our history. All the work for which we're recognised was conceived during this amazing period. It was a case of idea today, action tomorrow.

The lesson for any budding social entrepreneur is clear. Use the freedom of this early period to innovate and create. Don't blow this unique early period for it will never come again!

Seek advantage over bigger, more bureaucratic rivals by your fleet of foot. Don't spend your very early period at a laptop writing policies and procedures. While you're a baby organisation, and it's just you and your cornerstones, you don't really need to. Sure, you may need some very specific policies and procedures just to operate within the law (for example Criminal Records Bureau checks, equal opportunities, health and safety, child protection, basic employment policies). But you don't need to spend a lot of time or energy on this. The web is full of sample polices that you can adapt for your own purposes. No need for policy committees or working groups, just cut and paste!

> *Don't blow this unique early period for it will never come again!*

Likewise, you don't need to spend lots of money on the best laptops or workspace. You probably can't afford them anyway. Our first office was in a run-down community centre, which we shared with a local samba band (not a very good one either!). The baby period is a special time, a one-off window of opportunity. Make the most of it.

Before we move on, this would be a good time for a bit of reflection: what do you want to achieve in your first couple of years?

Growing pains

Wisdom is nothing more than healed pain.

Robert Gary Lee, American author

All this chaos is fine while you're a baby organisation. However, once the baby starts to become a growing child, the lack of structure stops being fine. In fact, it rapidly turns from an advantage to a handicap. When does this happen? I put it at 10 employees. You've gone through dreaming and acting. You are now into building a sustainable, possibly scaleable organisation.

At this point, you need to make a big step change in terms of policies, systems and structure. It's hard to convey how suddenly the positives associated with a new organisation can quickly become negatives. If you fail to notice that the baby is out of nappies and carry on as before, you're suddenly exposed to all sorts of risks. And you are in no way ready for the next major period of your organisation's life. At best, you will struggle. At worst, this can lead to your early demise, as it so nearly did with us at Speaking Up.

Two years after I jacked in my day job, Speaking Up had five staff. During the next three years it grew from five to twenty-five. Even though it was abundantly clear that we were out of our baby phase, I refused to develop the necessary infrastructure of systems, policies and processes for the new organisation. So we ended up with extremely weak processes for financial control, no human resources support, no IT support, a poor working environment, the wrong insurances, few job descriptions or employment contracts, accounts that didn't add up and unnecessary risk in our work with clients.

How did this hurt us? Well, new staff just wouldn't put up with this sort of thing. Many felt personally compromised by the shambolic way we operated. Others felt resentful at our lack of apparent care over things like health and safety, and employment law. The fall-out from this was very bad for us. We had to deal with an employment tribunal, a couple of people leaving the organisation because they felt disgusted at the way it was run, a big drop in quality, and an increasing reputation for being erratic and unprofessional. By 2002, although we had achieved a great deal in terms of innovation and had won the coveted Guardian Charity Award, we were, in many respects, at our lowest ebb.

By 2002, although we had achieved a great deal in terms of innovation and had won the coveted Guardian Charity Award, we were, in many respects, at our lowest ebb.

If I could go back in a tardis to 1998, two years after I gave up my job to run Speaking Up, I would do things very differently. I had made mistakes. As a founder, I was still in love with being little. I didn't want to accept that the romance of the early years was over. I expected all the new people to just sort things out and work like Trojans, as we all did early on. I was, quite wrongly, worried that bringing in systems, policies and procedures would kill our entrepreneurial spirit. People who asked for a more professional culture and a bit of structure and sanity annoyed me. I saw them as 'jobsworths'. I just didn't get it. They were right, I was wrong.

So, what do *you* need to do yourself once your venture has gone through the baby stage?

The first thing is to stop and reflect on where you're at. Just step back and celebrate what you've achieved in those precious first years.

Then, soberly acknowledge that it is over. Accept that the baby has grown up and that you've got to change your approach. This will be a big psychological step for you as a founder, but don't duck it, like I did. Heather Wilkinson, of Striding Out, puts it nicely: 'As your business grows … it's no longer just about you and your ideas, it's about your team and their engagement in the development of the business'. Tim West, of *Social Enterprise Magazine*, says it will be less about 'doing the business and more about strategy, marketing, meeting and winning – or at least, that's the ideal, but it's bloody difficult letting go!'

On a more practical level, there are a number of things that you need to attend to urgently.

1. Sort out the structure of your organisation

The chances are that any structure you have will have evolved incrementally. The odds on it being fit for purpose to go forward are extremely low. People's roles will need to be clarified, as you'll all have been multi-tasking so far. Everyone will have elements within their jobs that don't sit well together. I remember clearly taking the task of 'going to the bank every week' out of my job description, with much relief. You'll probably need to re-title certain roles and re-write (or write for the first time) everyone's job description.

You'll need to introduce some hierarchy and lines of accountability. Without a sense of structure new people, who weren't part of your founding team, tend to be uncomfortable. As the founder, you'll probably, at this point, need to look at your own role and call yourself something like 'Chief Executive', however much you dislike fancy titles.

The more people I ask, the more I realise I'm not alone in this issue of role clarification at this stage of the venture.

Like me, Rob Harris of Advocacy Experience had to pitch in and deliver front line services and do administration work in poor conditions. Now, as he reflects on his changing role and the structure of his organisation develops further, he observes that 'my role is purely strategic, without delivery or operational management'.

For Jonathan Senker of Advocacy Partners, the act of clarifying his role was very comforting: 'I have colleagues who are far better at aspects of our work than I am and I don't need to understand everything'.

Luljeta Nuzi of Shpresa also found her role changing as her organisation grew: 'When I started I was just running without looking where I was stepping and how dangerous it was. Now I have to run, I have to watch and I have to let it go and this is the most difficult thing to do'. Ogunte's Servane Mouazan, on the other hand, has more responsibilities but also 'more skills and more eagerness to learn and share what I've gone through'.

Role clarification is a great task to do on an away-day. It gets everyone involved and widens the sense of ownership people have over the way the organisation is going. If you have trustees who have some experience in this area, invite them too. The outcome of this process is that you have a bunch of people who are clear about their roles and know what's expected of them. With a named boss they know who they can call on for support and to whom they are accountable. Most people need this kind of clarity. In terms of the positive effect this has on morale and retention, this is a great investment of time.

2. Introduce new processes

In the baby organisation, people intuitively do things in the same way. You can deal with most issues informally, a bit like you can in a family. As soon as it grows, people need processes to guide them. When I say processes, I mean an agreed way of doing things, which is written down, with which everyone is expected to comply.

Your processes will cover a very wide range of things from the way you run your finances, through to how you employ and support staff and how you deliver services. Processes enable people to know what they are doing. They make your organisation more efficient by ensuring a degree of uniformity and consistency. They give your people confidence and certainty. Without them you get duplication and confusion and, worst of all, unnecessary risk.

So what processes do you need to get right first?

Financial processes

If you don't control your finances, they will control you. There's a lot more about this in the finance chapter but, for lots of reasons, you need to get financial processes right as early as you can. If you don't, you run the risk of insolvency, or accusations of impropriety. As a founder, you need to understand how important it is that your growing organisation is seen to be solid in terms of its financial management. If there's the slightest feeling out there that your finances are badly managed, your own personal reputation is at risk. This is because that tiny minority who do fiddle the books tend to use poor financial management as a smokescreen.

Here is a short list of financial procedures that you need to implement if you already haven't. There are now a number of computer packages on the market that enable you do most of these processes on your PC or laptop.

- **Expense claim processes** – These must include signed authorisation from two people, preferably you and a trustee.
- **A monthly bank reconciliation statement** – This needs to be shared with yourself and your chair.
- **A cash flow prediction for the year ahead** – This must be adjusted with each month.

- **A budget for the financial year** – This needs to outline expected income and spending.
- **Monthly management accounts** – These must include variations against your budget.
- **Invoicing of debtors** – You need a process for the prompt sending of invoices to customers and for pursuing unpaid invoices.
- **Payment of creditors** – You need a process for the payment of invoices within a 30-day period.
- **Recording of transactions** – You need a process for the safe-keeping of all invoices sent and received.
- **Payroll** – You need a system for doing payroll each month, ensuring that the Inland Revenue receives tax and NI for each of your employees.
- **Year-end accounts** – You need a system for doing 'year-end' accounts, which summarise the previous 12 months' financial activity.

Employment processes

In the early days, when there are just a couple of you, it doesn't actually feel like you're 'employed' in the traditional sense. However, this soon changes once you need to hire staff or use large numbers of volunteers.

Employing people is, in itself, a bigger risk than most people realise. But it's a risk you can't really avoid if you want to get anything done. You need to limit your risk by ensuring that your employment processes are robust.

> *You need to limit your risk by ensuring that your employment processes are robust.*

Sound employment practices are crucial for two reasons. First, you need happy, motivated staff if you're going to be successful. Second, employment law in the UK is very tight in terms of how you have to deal with staff problems, changes in their working practices or redundancy.

Below are the things that you definitely need to have sorted as your venture exits the baby phase.

Job descriptions

These need not be big, long documents, but everybody needs to have a piece of paper that states what they are at work to achieve. This needs to be precise enough to make expectations clear but not so detailed as to list every possible task. Remember, as a smaller organisation, you will need people to be flexible.

Whatever you do, don't let any of your staff start work without a job description. If you ever need to take action to improve their performance, they may claim they were never given one and you'll be powerless to do anything. Job descriptions can also state required behaviours and attitudes as well as tasks. Include these, because attitude is just as important in service-based organisations. Keep a copy of everyone's job description filed away safely.

Contracts

A contract of employment sets out key terms and conditions. It is best to get this signed before somebody starts or it tends to get forgotten about. A contract contains what an employee can expect of you and what you can expect of them. Therefore, you need signatures – yours and the employee's are essential for it to be valid. You can download sample contracts from the web (www.businesslink.gov.uk) but, better still, obtain one from a human resources advice service. In smaller organisations with unstable funding, contracts are extremely important, as it may be not be possible to redeploy staff if you lose funding. Without a contract you will be in a weaker position in any dispute with an employee. Even if a staff member hasn't actually signed a contract, they are considered in law to have a contract with you. So don't think that an employee has no contract if he or she hasn't signed one. All you need to know here is that you should issue one for every employee. Make sure they keep a signed copy and you keep one too. About five percent of my working life has been spent dealing with problems arising from bad or non-existent contracts with staff. Save yourself the trouble by getting this right first time.

> *Save yourself the trouble by getting this right first time.*

Policies on sick pay, holiday, compassionate leave and maternity pay

There are certain statutory minimums around most of these policies that you must observe, but it is up to you if you want to offer over and above these. These policies need to be included in an employment handbook which you issue to all staff. You may also want to include them in your contract of employment. For guidance on maternity pay go to www.dwp.gov.uk/lifeevent/benefits/statutory_maternity_pay.asp. For sick pay go to www.direct.gov.uk/en/Bfsl1/BenefitsAndFinancialSupport/DG_10018786.

Policies on supervision and annual appraisal

It is good practice to offer all employees formal supervision and annual appraisal. Supervision should take place a minimum of four times a year, but you'll probably want to do it monthly or two-monthly. Once completed, supervision notes need to be signed by both the employee and the supervisor, a copy given to the employee and a copy filed in the employee's personal file. The same applies to an appraisal. It sounds obvious, but keep all supervision notes locked in a safe place. Sample templates for appraisals can be found at www.businessballs.com/performanceappraisals.htm.

Policies on performance and disciplinary procedures

You can be almost certain that at least one of the people you employ in the first five years will seriously underperform – or worse. Expect this. When it happens, the main thing is to deal with it. Get it right and you'll either improve the person's performance or you'll be able to release them fairly. Get it wrong, even in a relatively minor way, and you run a big risk of a claim for unfair dismissal and a big fine by an employment tribunal. I speak from experience, having had one such incident a year for each of the last 10 years.

Again, your policies need to reflect what is legally required and you should get advice on this from an HR adviser. Such advisers will send you templates for this and all the other policies mentioned. You just need to customise them, put your own logos on and use them whenever such issues arise.

I strongly recommend that you sign up to an employment law advice service. It's not a lot of money for what you get. Not only do they offer helpline support during a crisis, they will, if you follow their advice to the letter, represent you at no extra cost and pay any fine issued by an employment tribunal. These are just three advice services you could try: Peninsula (www.peninsula-uk.com), One Click HR (www.oneclickhr.com), or Empire HR (www.empirehr.com).

Training and personal development policy

The best organisations support the personal development of their staff. It is sensible to set out your intentions in your employee handbook. We go as far as to create personal development plans for all employees and to give each staff member a £500 annual budget to spend on their own development. This sounds a lot but it's not, considering what it costs to replace staff.

Employee handbook

This brings together the standard information about working for you so that employees have everything in one place. This includes a standard contract of employment (left blank) and all of your staff-related policies.

Employment files

You will need one of these for every employee. They should all be stored in one place under lock and key. Each file should contain a signed copy of the employee's contract, their current job description, all notes from supervisions and appraisals and records of holidays taken. If you don't want to lose them, never remove them from the office.

Service delivery

If you're a social venture, you're probably delivering some kind of service to people. Depending on your sector, there are likely to be a number of regulations governing organisations that deliver services. If you're working with vulnerable adults or children, then you will definitely be affected by a high number of requirements, many of which will be set out to you in service level agreements or contracts.

Such regulations have grown in number in the UK during the last 10 years. In the event of something going wrong, any failure to comply could have a serious effect on your organisation. Therefore, it is vital to invest time and energy in ensuring you're 'fit for purpose' for delivering services.

This involves more than having particular policies. It can also mean having a certain level of accreditation or training for staff, or protocols (agreed procedures) around working with particular groups.

Here are some examples of things you may need to get sorted out:

- Child protection policies if you work with under-18s;
- Public liability insurance to cover claims against your staff or organisation;
- Criminal Record Bureau checks for all staff;
- Training in best practice for protection of vulnerable adults or children;
- Equal opportunities policies;
- Lifting and handling policy;
- Serious incident policy and protocol;
- Lone worker policy.

3. Define your organisational culture

The companies that survive longest are those that work out what they uniquely can give to the world – not just in terms of growth or money but their excellence, their respect for others, or their ability to make people happy. Some call those things a soul.

Charles Handy, management writer

As the organisation grows from baby to child, the culture changes with it. Gone are the days when you all stayed until midnight to get a bid done. No longer do you all pile down the pub and dream about the future. You're now into another phase. You'll need new people and, while they may never share your intense passion, you'll have to decide what you require from them in terms of attitudes and values. This is the time to define your organisational culture.

When I did this with Speaking Up (three years too late), our entrepreneurialism ranked highly and our professionalism ranked very low in terms of how we saw ourselves at the time. When we thought about the *future*, the two ranked equally. We ended up with a values statement that said we were entrepreneurial, passionate and professional. This, belatedly, replaced the earlier culture of spontaneity and informality.

As your venture grows, this new statement of values will be a big part of your 'brand'. Your brand is what you are known for. It could be your energy, your entrepreneurialism or your can-do attitude. Whatever it is, write it large in the minds of your new employees.

What is your organisational culture?

This is a really good exercise to help you find out. Sit down with your current team and follow these steps:

- Working individually, write on a piece of paper the five core attributes of your organisation.
- Ask each person to rank each attribute from one to five (one = most important).
- Throw all the papers into the middle and see what you've got.
- Add up the scores, then group them in rank order. The lowest scored items indicate your 'highest values'.

When you've done this, do it again, but this time asking what you think the organisation's culture needs to look like in the future, when there are more of you and you need to bring people in to help. You'll probably produce a slightly different list.

From this, you should try to put together a statement of your values as an organisation. It should be very short, memorable and included on every job advert, job description and every screensaver in your organisation.

As for Speaking Up...

Speaking Up's experience had a happy ending. After three years of treating my child like a baby, the penny eventually dropped and we made a conscious decision to refocus the organisation on improving its infrastructure.

I put growth and development on hold for a while and spent a lot of energy securing the kinds of changes outlined above. The benefits were enormous. In doing this, we:

- improved the morale of our staff and volunteers;
- secured improvements in the delivery of our services;
- reduced our risk of being sued for non-compliance with the law;
- finally got a grip on our finances, allowing us to plan properly for the future;
- restored the confidence of funders and partners;
- freed ourselves up to think about innovation again.

This process, though it came three years too late, was the key to us moving into a subsequent period of substantial growth.

DEALING WITH YOUR GROWING PAINS

Is it too much to ask you to see that far ahead, beyond your organisation's 'baby years'?

If you've already reached the time for change, are you able to acknowledge that it's happening, accept it and take the necessary actions?

- If you're ready to move on, then you need to say goodbye to being a 'boutique' business – forever.
- Buy an infrastructure – systems, processes and policies. If you don't like doing this, recruit someone who does.
- Remember, culture knits an organisation together. And you have a massive role in shaping it.
- When your baby starts turning into a child, make sure that the growing pains are no worse than they need to be.

Failing to plan is planning to fail.

Robert Schuller, pastor

13 From child to grown-up: scaling up

Greatness is not a function of circumstance. Greatness, it turns out, is largely a matter of conscious choice, and discipline.

Jim Collins, American management writer

Most charities and social businesses are inherently small and localised, probably employing no more than 10–20 people. There is nothing wrong with this. Indeed, in many respects, this is the ideal size in terms of controlling your costs and managing your organisation and its culture. If, however, you want to either up-scale your business or replicate it in new locations, I can tell you that expansion from being a small business (up to 25 people) to a medium-sized one (25–150 people) is an incredibly exciting experience. You see the tiny acorn you planted a few years earlier suddenly grow into a mighty oak. However, this will also be a hugely challenging experience. Do not underestimate this.

View from a social entrepreneur

What size of vehicle are you driving?

'When you ride a bicycle, you are flexible, pass the traffic easily, leave the cars and lorries behind you, keep feet on the pedals, get wet from the unpredictable weather. When you decide to drive a small car you need not just the car, you need petrol, you have to wait in the traffic but still you can turn very quickly, you can use different routes ... When you become a lorry God help you, you are limited in that you have to plan your journey carefully, you need lots of petrol, when you want to turn you have to plan well ahead because you can cause an accident. So we have decided to build a small car, and we'll be able to show other people how to build their own cars or maybe how to ride a bicycle first.' (Luljeta Nuzi, Shpresa)

If you thought start-up was hard, think again. Scaling up is tougher still because, unlike before, you're not in full control. It will also be a risky experience. You will have to spend a lot of money improving the infrastructure of your organisation before you know whether you can pay for it. It is no myth that growing businesses are the most vulnerable to insolvency.

> *Furthermore, scaling up will change your business forever.*

Furthermore, scaling up will change your business forever. You cannot be a 'boutique' business beyond a particular size. If you believe that you can replicate the virtues of a boutique business on a larger scale, stop dreaming. Indeed, your challenge will be to use the sheer scale of your new organisation to make up for the efficiency you will lose from ceasing to be small. Finally, you may find that, as an entrepreneur, you actually don't enjoy the task of scaling up nearly as much as you enjoyed the foundation period. Expansion of a business often signals the end of the line for the founding entrepreneur.

Heather Wilkinson of Striding Out reckons 'This is the time when you start working *on* the business as opposed to *in* the business. Scaling up the company requires investment, time, energy and resources and securing all these can be a difficult task while juggling the day-to-day dynamics of the business'.

For Doug Cresswell of Pure Innovations, there's a lot to lose. 'If you get this wrong you end up spreading the margarine too thinly and lose any existing quality already in place at the expense of growth. It's a tough, fine line, because in order to grow you need to get more great people on board. But new, great people are thin on the ground and can be expensive to attract into your business. You have to be clear how the next 'big thing' will be managed and integrated without dragging the existing business down. Sound due diligence is essential, if you get the resource issues wrong in your initial forecasting you could be heading for disaster.'

So, there are challenges to scaling up your business. Whether, according to Owen Jarvis of Aspire Support UK, it's 'lack of business skills and nous; lack of confidence that we can scale up', or sometimes, as Miles Hanson of Collaboration Company told me, it's as simple and as important as 'looking after myself properly and spending enough quality time with my family'.

Still interested in scaling up one day? Well, in that case read on ...

Ways to scale up a business

> **You will either step forward into growth or you will step back into safety.**
>
> *Abraham Maslow, American psychologist*

There are a number of ways to scale up a business. One is organic growth. This is simply about winning new orders and growing the base of clients for whom you work. Another is by franchising your business. This is where you, in effect, licence another entrepreneur to use your idea, business name and methods under a legal agreement. Quite a few well-known businesses, such as The Body Shop or Hertz, work this way. A third way is by acquisition, where you buy another business as a going concern and make it your own.

There are advantages and disadvantages to each of these approaches. The appropriateness of each model will depend on the nature of your business and the pace at which you seek to expand.

Model	Advantages	Drawbacks	Best suited to ...
Organic growth	You can choose the staff It is normally more gradual You are repeating what you know It is easier to integrate new work	It can be slow You carry all the risks associated with growth	Complex, difficult-to-replicate businesses Businesses that rely on a particular organisational culture to achieve results More slow-growing businesses
Franchising	You can grow rapidly You share risks and benefits with the franchisee You can achieve big economies of scale It helps to establish your business as a brand	You can lose control of the end product A franchise business that fails can affect the 'parent' company	Easily replicable businesses Businesses where a well-known brand really matters Businesses that need to reach 'critical mass' to succeed in the marketplace
Acquisition	You can grow rapidly You can dominate a sector The business is 'ready-made' and the risks lower Financial planning is easier	The existing culture can be resistant There are always unknowns, even in a well-researched business Money needs to be spent on integration	Businesses that need to quickly establish themselves as key players in a market Businesses that can achieve efficiency by buying existing businesses Businesses that are highly skilled in exporting their culture into existing companies

Critical success factors in scaling

A global study of 28 successfully up-scaled social enterprises by LaFrance Associates (2006)[1] identified seven critical success factors in successful scaling of social businesses. These are set out below.

1. Defining and adhering to core mission

Successful scale up depends, to a large extent, on the ability of an organisation to successfully transmit its mission into new projects and services. The mission also acts as a guide to decision-making about growth. In short, if new growth doesn't fit the mission, it will reduce the chances of organisational success.

2. Balancing control and flexibility

Scaling up successfully depends on getting the right balance in the relationship between the 'head office' location and new offices or services. Complex services require a tight model of control if they are to be replicated effectively. Fairly simple services, or services based on a loose model, do not need much oversight. Enterprises that have grown to scale have achieved the right kind of balance between control and flexibility.

3. Codifying what works

A business model that is clearly written down stands a far greater chance of being taken to scale successfully. A codified model consists of a documented programme, a statement of policies and procedures, and a statement of organisational structure and culture. This provides a blueprint for new sites to replicate the original programme. It identifies what is critical for success in a new service and allows the service to be tested against this.

4. Creating and perpetuating the culture

For up-scaling of a business to succeed, organisations must foster those aspects of their culture – values, behaviour and norms – that are critical to mission accomplishment. Many of the 28 organisations studied cited culture as the reason why they could attract talented staff and sustain high levels of performance and innovation.

5. Data

The ability to gather and use data was a critical factor in making good decisions about up-scaling social businesses. Successful enterprises were skilled in piecing together evidence of need, and making a case for development to potential investors and partners.

6. Resources

Organisations generating the money needed for growth were skilled at building new kinds of partnerships and relationships with supporters or connecting fundraising to mission. Fundraising in these organisations was as

---

[1] LaFrance Associates (2006) 'Scaling Capacities', LaFrance Associates.

much about getting people excited and involved in the mission as about one particular funding project.

7. Leadership and governance

Social businesses that have successfully gone to scale tend to have high-quality leaders and first-class governance arrangements. The board of directors plays a central role in the decision whether to scale, how to scale and in ensuring the resources are there to achieve growth. Effective boards provide what the organisation needs at a particular time in the scaling process. This could be strategic direction, connection to resources or the views of key stakeholders.

Growing too fast – a cautionary tale

At Speaking Up, we went for a mixture of organic growth and acquisition. This took us from a turnover of £500,000 to £3 million over a four-year period. Our challenge was to up-scale our advocacy services business. Of all our work-streams, we had chosen this one because advocacy services lent themselves most readily to up-scaling. Indeed, compared to our more complex specialised projects (our 'Lamborghinis'), it's relatively easy to transplant this 'Ford Fiesta' from one place to another.

Our vision was that we would win loads of new contracts and simply plonk our shiny new services on the ground in new locations around the UK. All we had to do was repeat what we had done in the first location. Or so we thought. But we had seriously underestimated the difficulties and costs involved in rapid growth. Even replicating a relatively simple business process to the same high standard we'd been achieving in our first location proved extraordinarily difficult.

All we had to do was repeat what we had done in the first location. Or so we thought.

This is particularly so if you are growing into new locations far away from where you began. There is something uniquely challenging about growing in this way. Napoleon once said that problems in new outposts of his empire could be predicted by how far they were away from Paris. Something similar can be said in business, too. But even if you're just adding new work in your current location, the issues are similar. New parts of a company will always feel, to some extent, separate from the earlier projects.

A big problem was the failure on our part to impose our culture on new locations and services. Geographic distance proved a real hindrance. From operating in four locations all within one region, we were operating in 18 separate locations all over England within a couple of years. Our culture quickly fragmented into two groups: people who were based in 'head office' and those from 'satellites', as people in new locations termed themselves.

This split culture was amplified by the fact that we were obliged in many places, under transfer of undertakings to previous employees (TUPE) arrangements, to employ staff who had worked for organisations that had lost contracts to us. Therefore, we immediately had two classes of employees –

those we had recruited and those who had been handed over to us. We had to spend a lot of time and energy integrating these people into our organisation.

The challenges of opening several new services at the same time also had a big effect on our ability to manage operations, deal with our customers and regulate quality. The IT we fitted didn't work. Our new offices were hastily sourced and then found wanting. Nobody had worked out, in proper detail, how to ensure business processes in the new locations gelled with those we already had in place. Complaints in new services soared as we tried, but failed, to get a grip on the quality of our services.

What we should have done was to impose our own 'change manager' in each location. Instead, in a number of the new locations we chose to retain managers from the old services. Unfortunately, we couldn't rely upon these people to transmit our culture and quickly get operational standards to the level we needed.

Over a two-year period, we ended up moving these managers on. However, if I had my time again, I would actually redeploy or pay off these people right at the start and bring our own people in.

Overall, our failure to integrate new services into the wider business cost us dearly in terms of lost reputation and strained relationships. It took us over a year to deliver what we said we would. Our customers stayed with us – but only just.

10 practical tips on how to scale up successfully
Any scaling up of your business will probably be at least twice as time-consuming, complicated and diverting as you'd imagine it would be.

1. First, ask yourself 'why growth?'
If you want to grow, give this some deep thought. Think about the optimum size for your organisation. Understand the benefits growth might bring. Be honest with yourself about your motives for growing. Is it about meeting social needs or it is about your needs as an entrepreneur? Consider the risks of growth versus remaining small. What do you stand to lose if you grow? Will you be any more sustainable as a larger organisation?

2. Carefully research new business development
While your time will be limited, don't rush into things. Experiment in new markets by running pilots or small partnership projects before sinking lots of cash into expansion. Remember that you'll have to add infrastructure before your sales or new funding comes in. It's important to know the strength of your market before going ahead, as you could end up with a small organisation that is saddled with the running costs of a larger one.

3. Plan your growth like a military operation
You have a window during the first three months of a new service in which to put everything into place. This is the time to 'flood' the new people with

everything needed to properly integrate them and their service into the wider organisation. We now use a 'start chart' to plan our growth. This says to the day what will happen during the first 100 days of the new service. We have found that failing to do this in the first three months causes the service to develop (or retain) a powerful sub-culture, which is often at odds with that of the wider organisation.

4. Recruit managers who will transmit the values of the organisation

Without 'cherry-picked' people leading new services, you lose all influence over the way new parts of your business will be run. Ideally, these managers should be people who already work for you. Where this isn't possible, they need to be personally selected and briefed by you. This means that their first loyalty will be to the organisation, not to the individuals they are leading – or their former employer. You will rely on this manager to model the behaviour, attitudes and values of the organisation and, where necessary, to impose an organisational line. For all the above reasons, you should almost always seek to reach a financial or redeployment agreement with an existing manager before the service goes live. There are exceptions to this, of course, but normally you will need to get your own person in there from the off.

5. Make your presence felt

Get out into new services yourself, as often as humanly possible, to champion the company's culture and values. Your presence as a founder has enormous value. You embody what the organisation stands for. People want to know what the organisation is all about. Turn up and tell them about your vision, your values and what you want from the team.

6. Get the specialists in

A new service is like a new house. Often things are missing or don't work. Therefore, you need to have short-term specialists on hand in a new location or service. It may be an expert from an existing service to harmonise business processes or simply to wire IT into the rest of the organisation. Today's HR manager will ensure that all staff are 'socialised' into the values of the organisation via induction and values training. If you get to 100 people, you need a full-time HR manager. Up to this point, hire an HR expert each time you add a new service and make do with an advice-line HR service.

7. Be directive at first

In new services people normally don't know what to do and require a lot of direction. Ensure that these people form the right habits. Don't just assume people will know how to do a good job. Indeed, assume they don't. The time for trust and empowerment is some time down the line, once they have learned the ropes.

8. Don't grow too fast

If you are doubling in size every year, there is a good chance that you're opening up too many new fronts at once. Make sure you are putting all your energy into new services. Don't dilute yourself to the point where you don't really know what is going on. If you do, you'll be in for some nasty surprises – and it will often be too late to do anything about them.

9. Review, review and review

The first year of a new project or service sets the tone for the next five, so it is important to be on top of it from the start. Ensure new services receive a lot of scrutiny and high-level input. Involve yourself personally in reviewing new work as it signifies the importance the organisation places on its new business.

10. Resource growth properly

Fact: bigger organisations are more expensive to run. If you plan to go beyond 20-or-so employees, then you need to factor in a big step change in your costs. The integration of new services is particularly costly in terms of time and opportunity costs. It is easy to under-resource growth to achieve a short-term surplus. The trouble is that these services then never really perform. A budget for growth needs to factor in much larger sums for items such as HR, IT, finance, admin, travel and organisational development. Things you could do without as a small business become essential items once you start to grow.

SCALING UP

Can you see your new business scaling up one day?

Or, do you think that, for your social business, staying small is the right thing to do?

- Scaling up is something that a relatively small number of businesses go on to do.
- Mission, culture and complexity are vital in scaling – ask yourself whether your venture really is replicable.
- You need to decide on the best method – branching or franchising. Both can succeed, both can fail.
- If you do take your business to scale, you could also become one of the small number of social entrepreneurs who have a global impact. If you are potentially one of these people, think hard about the messages in this chapter – then take them all over the world!

The three great essentials to achieve anything worthwhile are, first, hard work; second, stick-to-it-iveness; third, common sense.

Thomas Edison, inventor of the light bulb

14 Looking after number one

How am I going to live today in order to create the tomorrow I'm committed to?
Anthony Robbins, American personal development coach

This chapter isn't about how to be self-centred. It's about how to survive and grow as a social entrepreneur. One of the hardest things about this particular vocation is that you can quickly get tired, lonely and lost. While an entrepreneur is, by nature, a hardy specimen, even a cactus needs water. Therefore it is worth, very early on, giving some serious thought to your own support-needs.

A big piece of learning from a recent study for the School for Social Entrepreneurs (Chambers and Edwards-Stuart, 2007[1]) is the extent to which relationships with supporters contribute to the success of social entrepreneurs. This chapter looks at what is available to you, and at some techniques to ensure you avoid burning out. I start by looking at informal approaches and go on to look at some of the excellent formal support programmes now available to new social entrepreneurs.

Doing it yourself – informal approaches to your own support

Mentors

> *Mentoring is to support and encourage people to manage their own learning in order that they may maximise their potential, develop their skills, improve their performance and become the person they want to be.*
>
> Eric Parsloe, Director, Oxford School of Coaching and Mentoring

A mentor is a guide who can help you to create solutions to issues in your developing venture. A mentor should also help you to believe in yourself and boost your confidence. They should ask questions and challenge, while providing guidance and encouragement. Time with a mentor allows you to explore new ideas and to 'think aloud'. It is a chance to look more closely at your own development and skills.

Mentors give you a sense of partnership and they are people to whom you can turn during your 'dark nights of the soul'.

My own experiences and the interviews for this book have convinced me that a mentor is a vital piece in the jigsaw for any aspiring social entrepreneur. Mentors give you a sense of partnership and they are people to whom

[1] Charlotte Chambers and Fiona Edwards-Stuart (2007), 'Leadership in the Social Economy', School for Social Entrepreneurs.

you can turn during your 'dark nights of the soul'. At a time when your venture is entirely dependent on your decisions, a mentor can help you to clarify the issues and move ahead with confidence. In short, a good mentor combines the role of listener, adviser and friend.

Who would make a good mentor for you? There's no fixed concept of what a mentor should be like. I have had three mentors down the years, all entirely different. The key is that you should like and enjoy each other's company. Time together should feel really good. The chemistry has to be right. You should have enough points of intellectual connection but the focus needs to be on you and what you're seeking to achieve. You should be taking from your mentor, not directly giving. Their satisfaction comes from your success, not your listening or advice to them.

> **Mentor: someone whose hindsight can become your foresight.**
> *Unknown*

You can find a mentor in a number of ways. Start close to home. Would any of your directors or trustees make a good mentor? If not, try further afield in your own network of friends and associates. Look at former tutors, bosses or

colleagues. If nobody stands out, look at friends of friends. Put the word out though e-mail or social networking sites that you are looking for a mentor. There are, I have found, lots of great people out there who would love to be asked; people with a lifetime of experience who want to connect with somebody starting something new. I have found mentors for people in my teams incredibly easily.

Support networks

> **All men are caught in an inescapable network of mutuality.**
> *Dr Martin Luther King Jr, American civil rights campaigner*

As a social entrepreneur, you'll more than likely be a natural networker. One of the purposes of your network is to develop a hub of support around yourself. Not all networking needs to be about building your business. Some should be about sustaining you, as the person who is holding the business together. A group of supporters – people who believe in you and what you are doing – is important for you. This is not only for the 'leverage' this group can provide, but for the psychological benefit of knowing you have a group of fellow believers behind you.

Personally, I have found my support network to be absolutely critical. As a social entrepreneur, you go through many difficult times. It is vital to know there is a community of people who believe in you and what you are trying to achieve.

My support network has developed over time. It has steadily expanded to include other social entrepreneurs and, now, CEOs of charities. Time spent with people in this network isn't always high-value strategic networking. It is also about nurturing a personal eco-system in which you can thrive. Relationships inside your network are more reciprocal than that you will have with a mentor. You give at least as much as you take. But by helping others and being helped, you create a support system around yourself to which you can turn and which gives you an ongoing sense of being sustained.

> *It is vital to know there is a community of people who believe in you and what you are trying to achieve.*

Learning

> **I am always ready to learn although I do not always like being taught.**
> *Winston Churchill, British Prime Minister 1939–45 and 1951–5*

The desire and ability to learn has been identified as a key feature of successful social entrepreneurs. This doesn't necessarily mean formal learning but the desire to find out new information, develop new skills and look at things in new ways.

To do this requires an investment of time. However, in the early days of a new venture, time is the one thing you feel you don't have. But, whatever you do, make sure you invest in your own learning. Visit other organisations. Speak to people who have built businesses. Attend lectures and events. Go to an evening class. Do it all. My early learning included visits to social enterprises in the USA and Europe. I drank in the experiences of established social entrepreneurs. Later, I did an MBA with the Open University to help me get a grip on my growing organisation.

Even now, I spend hours and hours learning a month. The reason is that I bring all this back into Speaking Up. A handful of the things I have picked up through my learning have had a massive influence on the direction of the organisation. You'll find this too. A thirst for learning keeps you focused on the world and stops you from becoming inward-looking. All this is essential if your venture is going to become sustainable.

Views from the social entrepreneurs

How do you maintain energy during the hard times?

- 'I'd like to say, sex, drugs and rock and roll, but in all honesty I simply have to slog my way through the hard times, clocking up emotional debts with loved ones and colleagues to make sure I repay them tenfold during the good times.' (Owen Jarvis, Aspire Support UK)

- Thinking of the people we are trying to help, the big picture of a better society, and realising that I'd rather be doing this than a "normal" job!' (Martin Clark, Citylife)

- 'I like to keep super fit and run marathons so I go for a run ... in my dreams! In reality, I go home slump in front of the telly and watch anything really banal, drink red wine, feel worse and then bounce back like Tigger!' (Doug Cresswell, Pure Innovations)

- 'If I'm low mentally, through pressure of work, I'm low physically, and vice versa. So, in times of stress, I ensure an equivalent physical outlet – personally, I dig holes in the garden, uproot unwanted shrubs, remove turf, create flower borders, tend to my organic vegetable plot. For me, it's the only way to maintain the mental/physical balance.' (Mark Griffiths, Ideal Word)

- 'I have never seriously contemplated giving up, even in hard times, as I can't imagine a job I would love more.' (Karen Mattison, Women Like Us)

- 'The hard times and the adrenaline create the energy – the problem is maintaining the energy during the good times.' (Steve Sears, ECT Group)

Self-care

Habit # 7: Sharpen the Saw
Stephen Covey, American author of The 7 Habits of Highly Effective People

For the first three years of running Speaking Up, I pretty much abused myself. I worked up to 80 hours a week, lived on takeaway food and smoked cigarettes to calm my nerves. I lived alone in a bedsit and didn't have a long-term partner. (I wonder why?)

I did all this in the somewhat misguided belief that this level of discomfort was somehow necessary for success, a rite of passage, almost. The reality is that I made myself pretty ill and held back the organisation because I couldn't function at the level needed to move it to a more sustainable position.

My wake-up call came when my mental health got precariously bad and a few good people helped me to sort out my life. One of these, Katy, eventually became my wife. I got my hours down to no more than 50 a week. I went running every day, kicked the fags and the Red Bull, bought a house and made time in my life for myself. Strangely enough, I began to be much more effective at work, too.

I am telling this story as a warning to anyone who thinks that becoming a successful social entrepreneur means you have to be a masochist. You don't. While life will, without doubt, be a lot harder than that of a salary-taker, you really don't need to do what I did. Indeed, if you do, you may, ironically, be risking your new venture.

> *One of my friends advised me that my work would probably take a lifetime and that I should pace myself accordingly.*

My breakthrough came when I realised that I was one of the organisation's key assets. As such, I should maintain myself properly. One of my friends advised me that my work would probably take a lifetime and that I should pace myself accordingly. These were amazing words, which I shall never forget.

Structured support for new social entrepreneurs

> *Keep away from people who try to belittle your ambitions. Small people do that, but the really great make you feel that you, too, can somehow become great.*
>
> Mark Twain, American author

There are now a number of options for new social entrepreneurs in terms of structured learning and support.

School for Social Entrepreneurs

The School for Social Entrepreneurs (SSE) runs practical learning programmes aimed at developing the individual entrepreneur and their organisation. The SSE has now expanded beyond its base in Bethnal Green, London, and the network of SSEs around the UK continues to grow. Over 300 SSE Fellows have completed programmes around the country.

SSE believes that it is a combination of personal support and development, project knowledge and leadership skills that leads to the creation of sustainable social businesses. In SSE's experience, creating new organisations to address disadvantage is a personal process, so they offer personal as well as project support. It is also their experience that it is not theoretical learning but action learning that is the most effective for people leading social change. SSE believes that peer support and group learning are maximised by a diverse intake of students, leading a wide and inspiring range of projects.

> *... it is not theoretical learning but action learning that is the most effective for people leading social change.*

The SSE programme is open to entrepreneurial individuals who are serving communities. Students range from 19–74 in age; roughly half are women and half men, with a mix of educational experiences including those with no formal qualifications and others who are professionally or academically qualified.

UnLtd (www.unltd.org.uk)

Though better known as a source of funding for social entrepreneurs (see Chapter 6, 'Finding investment or funding'), UnLtd's Millennium Awards provide practical as well as financial support to social entrepreneurs in the UK. That's why you don't just get money from UnLtd. If you win an award you will get a complete package of support designed just for you, in addition to the financial support.

Striding Out (www.stridingout.co.uk)

This organisation was set up by Heather Wilkinson to help younger people to 'stride out' on their journey by providing a range of tailored support that was youthful, exciting and dynamic – and very unlike sitting in the classroom. They now also run Branching Out, to work with the over 30s, and Reaching Out, to work with hard-to-reach groups.

Striding Out offers the following support to social entrepreneurs:

- One-to-one coaching;
- Networking and learning events;
- Training and development workshops;
- Expert advice from professional advisers.

Their approach is to provide you with the right information, support and resources throughout the different stages of your business journey – whether you are exploring an idea, planning a business, have just launched a business, or you are planning to grow your business.

Golden nuggets from people who know

Naturally, I asked my dynamic and varied group of social entrepreneurs for their one golden nugget of advice to share with budding social entrepreneurs. I received some dynamic and varied answers – a few dos, but many don'ts. We all learn what we need to learn in different ways. Although I give you 20 clear advice themes in my final chapter, I can't help but share a few of these nuggets here, in relation to 'looking after number one'.

'Don't go into a social enterprise unless you are prepared to give 100%', said Phil Knibb, of Alt Valley Community Trust.

'Be sure you have something very worth doing and avoid mission drift', added Roger Wilson-Hinds, of Screenreader. In a similar vein, Karen Mattison, of Women Like Us, urges you not to 'reinvent yourself to fit with funding'. Streetshine's Simon Fenton-Jones puts it yet another way: 'By all means listen to advice but stay focused on your goals'. And Luljeta Nuzi of Shpresa backs him up: 'Don't allow others to direct your project, ask lots of people about something, but you make the decision'.

Not forgetting about this one: 'Don't grow too fast', says Mark Griffiths, of Ideal Word. He's supported by Shagufta Shahin, of Newham College: 'Don't plan on being big from the get-go! Start small, but think big. Don't work hard, work smart'.

There's something about a sense of realism: ECT Group's Stephen Sears suggests we try not to be unrealistic: 'Just because you want to create something it doesn't mean there is a real market for it'.

But I'm going to leave the last word to Owen Jarvis of Aspire Support UK: 'Avoid arrogance and self-righteousness – after all, why should anyone buy what you're selling? Who says the world does need to change in the way you say it does? There's no harm in unshakeable self-confidence, of course.'

LOOKING AFTER NUMBER ONE

Are you clear about the need to invest in your biggest asset – yourself?

Do you realise how vital this is – however talented and robust you are?

- Finding a mentor, building a support network and investing in your own learning are all absolutely critical success factors.
- You'll need support and access to ongoing learning if you are to make a success of your venture.
- Look after your physical and mental health.
- A healthy enterprise depends on a healthy you. Don't ever forget that.

Life is a series of experiences, each of which makes us bigger, even though it is hard to realise this. For the world was built to develop character, and we must learn that the setbacks and grieves which we endure help us in our marching onward.

Henry Ford, American founder of Ford Motor Company

15 Bringing it all together: 20 top tips for successful social entrepreneurship

A business has to be involving, it has to be fun and it has to exercise your creative instincts.
Sir Richard Branson, founder of Virgin

Throughout this book you've heard from a range of successful social entrepreneurs, including myself, on a range of issues, from finding investment through to how to maintain energy during the hard times. When I was researching the book, I became aware of a number of recurring pointers that would aid new entrepreneurs on their learning trajectory. Therefore, in this final chapter, I pull these together in the form of a vital '20 top tips' for new social entrepreneurs.

The 20 top tips

1. If you feel you want to do it, seize the day
Asked about their biggest single mistake, these were the answers from four social entrepreneurs:

- 'Not starting earlier!' (Richard Alderson, Careershifters)
- 'Waiting too long before going for it.' (Tim West, *Social Enterprise Magazine*)
- 'Staying safely with a large national charity for far too long, even though I hated being pushed around.' (Roger Wilson-Hinds, Screenreader)
- 'Taking too long to act on a new venture. We always knew we could recruit very successfully for employers but were worried about entering a very competitive market.' (Karen Mattison, Women Like Us)

So, 'seize the day' was the big theme coming from many people I spoke to. The lesson here is that the urge to take action is a sign, on some level, that the time is right to do so. There will never be a time when all your ducks are in a perfect line. Clearly, the message is: act now. Of all the mistakes that each of these people has made, their decision to delay start-up still figures largely in their minds.

> *There will never be a time when all your ducks are in a perfect line.*

2. Be true to yourself

- 'I enjoy the independence and opportunity to make a difference on my own terms.' (Simon Fenton-Jones, Streetshine)
- 'I was supporting creative entrepreneurs and was organising cultural events on a voluntary basis and someone one day told me I could make a living out of it. It didn't really feel like a "plunge", more like a very natural thing to do … like a relief!' (Servane Mouazan, Ogunte)

Many social entrepreneurs see their work as corresponding with their deepest purpose. All those interviewed positively relished the emotional rollercoaster that accompanied becoming a social entrepreneur. For them, autonomy and the thrill of the ride ranked much higher than their need for security or a predictable income.

The thing to learn here is that you need a particular temperament to take this path.

Therefore, you need to ask yourself if this is your 'true north' or just a flight of fancy? Will you truly enjoy the independence and adventure of social entrepreneurship? Do you have the necessary commitment to spend all your time making a new venture happen? Does this feel, on some level, like a personal necessity for you? If the answer to all these questions is 'yes', then you're on the right path.

The thing to learn here is that you need a particular temperament to take this path. If you don't enjoy having no safety net or a clear sense of what the future may hold, this is simply not the right thing for you. Being honest about this will save you a lot of heartache.

3. Be deeply passionate about your business

- 'Only do it if the business itself excites you! Something you would do for no money! If money comes along, that's a bonus!' (Shagufta Shahin, Newham College)
- 'Be yourself, let passion speak for you, read what they fund, be able to sell your project in no more than three minutes. Use different methods to make them feel what you feel.' (Luljeta Nuzi, Shpresa)
- '[What makes a successful social entrepreneur is] Passion. Individuality. Confidence but not arrogance. The refusal to accept no. The drive to achieve. The belief that you can change the world. The ability to question yourself. The clarity to move ahead with a plan – the ability to change the plan at every move.' (Tim West, *Social Enterprise Magazine*)

Every successful person I spoke to for this book was passionate about their business. They believed in it, lived it and loved it. Passion – and an ability to communicate it – seems to be a part of the DNA of a successful social entrepreneur. The passion of an entrepreneur inspires and attracts people to a business. It also motivates and energises those involved so that the business stands out from the crowd.

The learning point here is that not only do you personally need to have a strong feeling for what you are doing but you must communicate this to those around you.

4. Network like there is no tomorrow

- '[I] networked day and night, held my promises, nurtured connections with people I have met or supported, was honest when I couldn't deliver and always did my best to achieve something much better than what I was asked to do.' (Servane Mouazan, Ogunte)

Networks are powerful systems for mutual-aid that enable the individuals within them to achieve far more than they could on their own. All the research on social entrepreneurs says that they are star networkers. Our group were no different. A social entrepreneur understands, on a very intuitive level, that a set of great external relationships sits behind any successful venture. Social entrepreneurs also understand the power of networks to amplify or 'leverage' their influence, or to attract new resources or the right people into their organisation.

> *Social entrepreneurs also understand the power of networks to amplify or 'leverage' their influence, or to attract new resources or the right people into their organisation.*

5. Find a great support network

- 'Surround yourself with a brilliant team that complements your skills. Shadow successful people, get a mentor and a coach.' (Servane Mouazan, Ogunte)

Time and again, the social entrepreneurs I spoke to for this book talked about the need to get people around you who can support what you are doing. Foremost among these is a mentor or business coach. This is somebody to whom you enjoy talking to, who has a genuine interest in what you are doing and who is capable of offering a perspective on the key challenges facing you. On top of this, every social entrepreneur benefits from the informal support of a wide range of people. Knowing that there are people behind you is a big motivator. These might not be people with whom you spend much time but they need to be people on whom you can call should you need to.

6. Listen to advice but make your own decisions

- 'Acknowledge and accept that you are the person in charge and making the decisions; another way of saying this is don't respond to every bit of advice you get because most of the time the "adviser" hasn't been where you are.' (Rob Harris, Advocacy Experience)

From the word go, you'll probably have plenty of people offering their advice to you. Most people will give advice that reflects their own experiences and

> *So hear what advisers say, but make your own decisions based on what you think is right for your business now.*

prejudices, and not necessarily an appreciation of where you and your business are. Indeed, many advisers do not even listen properly before launching into their 'solution'. So hear what advisers say, but make your own decisions based on what you think is right for your business now.

Be selective about who you seek out for advice. If your advisers haven't done what you are doing, their advice may be useful but of limited value compared to time spent with somebody who has set up a business themselves. This is why I have always tended to avoid the kind of formalised business advice services staffed by people who have spent entire careers in the public sector. Ten minutes with a proper entrepreneur will be far more useful.

7. Write a great business plan

- 'I got people interested in TACT through well-thought-through proposals laced with inspiration and passion – with the beneficiary always at the centre.' (Bob Rhodes, TACT)
- 'To attract investment you need to present a compelling, clear, simple case for them to put money in.' (Richard Alderson, Careershifters)

A great business plan sits behind most great businesses. It will set out the vision of your organisation (the future you are working towards), the mission

> *Someone reading a good business plan will look up from the page feeling informed and inspired.*

(how your organisation is going to create that future) and the goals of the company. It will also set out your 'business model'; the particular methods you will use to create that future. It will be compelling, costed and credible. Someone reading a good business plan will look up from the page feeling informed and inspired. If it's really good, they may even want to come and work for you or invest some money themselves.

8. Earn trust

- 'Don't promise anything you can't deliver. Be frank and straight. Be nice to people; nobody likes to work with a sourpuss!' (Shagufta Shahin, Newham College)

Personal integrity is a must-have quality for any social entrepreneur. Nearly always, you are asking people to take a gamble on you, be it as a funder, an employer or a customer. To maintain that trust you have to deliver and show that you merited the risk that somebody has taken on you.

9. Live and breathe the business during year one

- 'There are no luxuries or perks – you may well be the whole of the business: tea-maker, post boy, letter-writer, accountant, managing director, business strategist, world-changer.' (Mark Griffiths, Ideal Word)
- 'Never underestimate the time commitment it will involve.' (Owen Jarvis, Aspire Support UK)

While it is important not to put your mental health at risk, it is extremely important that your main focus during your first year is the business. If you think it can be part of a 'work-life balance', think again. That may have been so in your old job but, in a new business, you can be assured that this will go out of the window. Year one (and probably two) is never balanced. It is a time during which your family, friends, hobbies and interests will all come second.

What makes this bearable is the passion you will feel for this new 'baby' in your life. Added to this is the fact that within a year or two things should have settled down a bit. But even then, the neatly compartmentalised life of a salary-taker will be gone for good. Work and life will never feel separate again.

10. Keep on top of your cash flow

- 'Above all, you are a manager of cash flow. Whatever you do, make offerings to the god of cash flow. Do anything to appease him ... short of compromising your values, of course.' (Mark Griffiths, Ideal Word)

While it is possible, from a fairly early time, to find people to do your book-keeping, it is vitally important for social entrepreneurs to be good at dealing with cash flow. For cash is the lifeblood of any business and a single lapse of attention on cash flow can be enough to put a great new venture into big trouble. Sure, leave the actual task to the bean-counters but never, ever, lose sight of the financial position of the business.

11. Never stop thinking about customers

- 'It takes clear communication from the beginning of a working relationship – managing expectations, offering fair pricing, living up to our own company values of honesty, trust, friendship and idealism, and always, always, delivering the goods. Then, not disappearing over the horizon but making sure that you're always on people's radars.' (Mark Griffiths, Ideal Word)

Customers are the oxygen of any business. They are hard to win and easy to lose. You win customers by being better, cheaper, nicer or easier to deal with than other people, or some combination of all of these. Organisations that live for their customers tend to be successful. They sink their best energy into keeping customers incredibly happy. Organisations that

Organisations that obsess with internal issues have little energy left for customers who slowly but surely drift away.

obsess with internal issues have little energy left for customers who slowly but surely drift away.

As a social entrepreneur, in the early days, you need to ensure your customers are the most important people in your life. Their needs should come only just below those of your partner and kids. By becoming your customer they have taken a risk on you and it's up to you to look after them.

12. Find the right people for your business

- 'I look for people who are hard working, positive, creative, fun, dynamic, able to think laterally, don't count the minutes or the pennies!' (Shagufta Shahin, Newham College)
- 'Integrity, creativity, self-reliance, great people skills and a passion for our mission are some of the key characteristics I look for.' (Bob Rhodes, TACT)

All the people interviewed for this book invested considerable energy in identifying and recruiting talent. All realised that their businesses would only be as good as the people they hired to work in them. The big message coming from the group is to aim very high, to employ only the very best people and to recruit on attitude as much as qualifications. A passion for the business ranks high on most people's 'wanted' list.

13. Remember that you need to make a profit if you are also to help people

- 'Don't forget about the "business" of social business.' (Richard Alderson, Careershifters)
- 'This is one of the hardest things, but ultimately I have to put financial goals first or else we'll all be out of a job.' (Simon Fenton-Jones, Streetshine)

Social entrepreneurs are usually really good at creating social outcomes. Our backgrounds tend to be in the caring professions. Our base motivation is social change rather than creating large, thriving businesses. For this reason, a lot of social businesses over-deliver on the social side but under-deliver in business terms.

Remember that to do good, you must also do well as a business.

However, in the long run, this results either in closure, or, at best, an inability to develop the organisation. It is vital, therefore, to set a reasonable balance between social and financial outcomes. This isn't to sa, you will need to make decisions that hurt your beneficiaries in order to make a profit. But to put short-term social outcomes ahead of financial sustainability is plain silly. Yet it happens all the time in social businesses – meaning, in effect, these organisations fail to develop and grow. Remember that to do good, you must also do well as a business.

14. Make sure you do the boring things right

■ 'Not getting certain basic things done – in our case sorting our company status – caused big problems later down the line. It's amazing how much trouble can be caused by failing to do fairly simple things in a timely way.' (Owen Jarvis, Aspire Support UK)

Amid the buzz of the early days of a social business there are some spirit-crushingly boring tasks that are likely to fall to you to do. Some of these are not critical (e.g. doing the petty cash every Friday) but some are, and you just have to do them. These include: annual insurances for the business and your premises; yearly tax returns; yearly returns to Companies House and the Charities Commission; monthly cash-flow statements, a monthly bank reconciliation statement; the cash book each month; quarterly VAT (if you sell VAT-able items); monthly payroll (if you employ staff); and written reports back to funders or customers whenever they are requested.

Failure to do any of these creates massive risks for your business that you could eliminate in a couple of hours holed up with a pot of tea and packet of Jammy Dodgers.

15. Find a first-class manager to help you up-scale your business

■ 'The real challenge as you grow in size is making sure you keep the integrity and values of the business. Making sure everyone in a tiny team knows what the business is about is easy ... keeping that true in a bigger organisation requires brilliant communication and careful recruitment!' (Karen Mattison, Women Like Us)

Moving out of the baby phase and building an infrastructure of systems, processes and culture is one of the biggest challenges for most social entrepreneurs. This is because it calls upon a different set of skills from those required during start-up. That is why it is important, at this stage, that you bring in a first-class manager who can focus on systems and processes. You can then focus on the thing you are best at – promoting the vision, values and aspirations of the business both internally and externally.

16. Understand that failure is a staging-post to success

■ 'There will be setbacks, but because you enjoy the business, you will want to do it anyway. If you don't basically like what you're doing, or you're doing it for the wrong reasons, then setbacks can finish you.' (Shagufta Shahin, Newham College)
■ 'Don't assume you will get everything right first time, because sadly you won't. It's as inevitable as "death and taxes".' (Rob Harris, Advocacy Experience)

Social entrepreneurs have a way of coping with setbacks. Quite simply, they 'reframe' them as opportunities to learn from or difficulties yet to be overcome. Seldom do they see setbacks as fatal or a reason to give up. Many successful social entrepreneurs have, at some stage, experienced a major business failure. Indeed three of the six ventures I have set up no longer exist!

The big message here is that, at some stage you will fail. You won't be able to avoid this because you're only human. What you will be able to control is your own response to it. You can, as I have seen many people do, simply pack up and get a job. Or you can brush yourself down, learn from what went wrong and start again. People who eventually succeed choose to do the latter.

17. Hold on to the vision

- 'Key qualities I see are Vision, Self-Belief, Perseverance, Creative/Problem Solving Thinking, Integrity!' (Bob Rhodes, TACT)
- 'I see a major quality of social entrepreneurs as Vision and the ability to draw in the right people around it.' (Richard Alderson, Careershifters)

Amid the difficult day-to-day reality of establishing a social business, it is really easy to lose sight of the vision that first inspired you. The fight for survival can very quickly become an end in itself. While survival is worth fighting for, it is also important that you view your big decisions through the prism of your mission. 'Is this decision going to help or hurt the people we set ourselves up to support?' is still the key question to be asked when facing the difficult questions.

Navigating the moral dilemmas thrown up by difficult business decisions or the imperatives of sound operations management is made easier when you have a deep grasp of your vision. A shared understanding of organisational vision, particularly within your management team, creates a framework through which to assess opportunities and to make choices, be these strategic or operational.

18. If it moves, measure it – embrace social accounting

- 'Auditing the difference you make to people's lives is just as important to the long-term sustainability of a social business as anything else you do.' (Owen Jarvis, Aspire Support UK)

If you think you are making a difference, it isn't enough just to proclaim this and wheel out a few stories in your annual report. 'Social accounting' – or measurement of what you are achieving for people and society – is set to become as important as financial accounting when it comes to deciding which organisations receive investment and funding.

Social accounting means being able to cost your outputs and outcomes for people in pounds and pence. It means being precise about the value you are adding and the savings your organisation is creating for the state and wider society. This is all a long way from the feel-good factor that many social-purpose organisations rely upon to demonstrate their worth.

19. Realise when it is time to move on

- 'When things no longer feel in the flow.' (Richard Alderson, Careershifters)
- 'When you think that you have done all you can do; when other opportunities are calling out; when others hint that you should change tack.' (Tim West, *Social Enterprise Magazine*)

Every social entrepreneur has a natural 'shelf-life' with a business before the time arrives for them to leave. The art is to either move on before you cause a crisis in the growing business, or to up your skills to fit the new needs of the business as it matures.

Remember, the thing that made you a great social entrepreneur won't necessarily make you a good CEO. This is one reason so many founders get out fairly early. Generally speaking, people who run things are different animals from people who set them up. And, unless you are fairly unusual, you won't enjoy running things nearly as much as you did setting them up.

According to the people interviewed for this book, the decision to leave will be an intuitive one: when things just don't feel the same any more; being able to hear the 'inner voice'. Or, in the words of Rob Harris, 'When it's plain obvious that it's all over'.

20. Look after your number one asset – yourself

- 'How do I maintain energy? Coffee, music, pretending to try and keep fit, enjoying my children, reminding myself that I really believe in what I do.' (Tim West, *Social Enterprise Magazine*)
- 'To maintain myself I switch off the computer and go to the restaurant; I do something different. I make sure I am kind to myself!' (Servane Mouazan, Ogunte)

Unlike most people, social entrepreneurs do not have a boss to look out for them. Nor do many have an 'off' button. Therefore, self-preservation (in the nicest sense) will be a necessity. This is not only important for your own well-being, it is also essential for your business. If you get burnt-out or ill, then the business will have little hope of a future.

In a very real sense, you are the number-one asset of the organisation.

In a very real sense, you are the number-one asset of the organisation. For this reason, you need to be careful with yourself. This means eating well, sleeping enough, taking exercise and keeping a record of how long you are working. A regular 70-hour week is probably going to cause you some serious damage!

Bringing it all together

These 20 tips bring this book to a conclusion. After reading them and the other chapters, I hope you feel it has repaid the time you have given to it. The intention has been to inspire, inform and engage you in your journey towards social entrepreneurship. However, as the book's subtitle suggests, it is also a no-fibbing, hard-headed and honest account of what is really involved in social entrepreneurship, told through the accounts of people who have been there. If it has helped you, I am glad. That has been my purpose. Now it's your chance to change the world. Good luck!

Index